"Ché Ahn's abiding passion t
and presence of God's Spiri̇ ̇ ̇
truth of God's glory, he points toward the personal realities and
practical leadership responsibility confronting each of us today.
Here are insights to move our thinking beyond the 'show' of
churchmanship to the 'glow' of vital New Testament dynamics,
without which the genuine 'weight of glory' cannot flow into
our souls and our congregations."

> —**Jack W. Hayford**, chancellor, The King's College and Sem-
> inary; founding pastor, The Church On The Way
> (Van Nuys, Calif.)

"Some go after the seemingly elusive realm of the glory of God
without emphasizing character at all. Worse, many live their
Christian lives as though this realm does not even exist. But the
Holy Spirit is bringing the realms of the power of God and the
fruit of the Spirit together. Ché Ahn, in his majestic book *When
Heaven Comes Down*, brings us the best of both worlds. The
glory of the Lord will cover the earth as the waters cover the
seas. Join Ché and a growing throng of other hungry believers
who quest for the presence of God, the power of Christ, intimacy
and holiness to release maximum impact in the earth today. You,
too, can have a visitation of a glorious kind!"

> —**James W. Goll**, Encounters Network; author, *The Seer, The
> Coming Israel Awakening, Prayer Storm* and many others

"You may be like me. *The glory of God* is a phrase I use constantly. But if you asked me to write a paragraph defining 'the
glory of God,' I would be stumped. No longer! Ché Ahn has
written not a paragraph but a whole book, pulling back the
curtains to help us not only to understand the glory of God,
but also to experience it as we turn the pages. *When Heaven
Comes Down* will take you into an entirely new realm of intimacy with God."

> —**C. Peter Wagner**, chancellor, Wagner Leadership Institute

"The words Moses uttered millennia ago still resound in the heart of every believer today: 'Lord, show me Your glory!' (Exodus 33:18). Don't you want to see, taste and experience the glory of God for yourself? In his new book, Ché Ahn gives us glimpses into God's glory. Through the Scriptures and present-day examples, Ché examines many aspects of this important subject, not only so that we can pursue a personal experience, but for the greater purpose of seeing God's glory transform cities and nations for expanding the Kingdom. You will be enlightened and encouraged in your pursuit of God as you read this book."

—**Jane Hansen Hoyt**, president/CEO, Aglow International

"Ché Ahn has written a wonderful book. There is nothing just like it because he connects the glory of God with God's right order and alignment with apostolic and prophetic restoration. The book is a faith builder that inspires us to seek Him for more of His glory-presence. Be inspired, transformed and reoriented as you read."

—**Daniel Juster**, director, Tikkun International, Jerusalem

"Glory is not just our destiny; it is meant to be our present experience. Ché has been a carrier and courier of glory for the past two decades. Drawing on his many supernatural experiences, he gives this profound and weighty subject easy access. As I read it, I found myself wanting more of God's glory in and around me. *When Heaven Comes Down* pulls back the veil of mystery and hands us keys for increasing the glory of God manifested in everyday life. Ché is one of the apostolic leaders of this present move of God, and his down-to-earth style and real-life stories have renewed my own motivation to seek after yet more divine glory in my everyday journey."

—**Charles Stock**, senior pastor, Life Center Ministries
(Harrisburg, Pa.); apostolic team member,
Harvest International Ministries

When Heaven Comes DOWN

Other Books by Ché Ahn

When Heaven Comes DOWN

Experiencing God's Glory in Your Life

CHÉ AHN

FOREWORD BY ROLLAND AND HEIDI BAKER

Chosen

a division of Baker Publishing Group
Grand Rapids, Michigan

Published by Chosen Books
A division of Baker Publishing Group
P.O. Box 6287, Grand Rapids, MI 49516-6287
www.chosenbooks.com

Printed in the United States of America

Library of Congress Cataloging-in-Publication Data
Ahn, Ché, 1956–
    When heaven comes down : experiencing God's glory in your life / Ché Ahn ; foreword by Rolland and Heidi Baker.
        p.   cm.
    Includes bibliographical references.
    ISBN 978-0-8007-9479-8 (pbk.)
    1. Glory of God—Christianity. 2. Spirituality. I. Title.
BT180.G6A36 2009
248.2—dc22   2009024428

09   10   11   12   13   14   15   7   6   5   4   3   2   1

In keeping with biblical principles of creation stewardship, Baker Publishing Group advocates the responsible use of our natural resources. As a member of the Green Press Initiative, our company uses recycled paper when possible. The text paper of this book is comprised of 30% post-consumer waste.

To Lou Engle
Prophet, Intercessor, Covenant Friend

Contents

Contents

Foreword

As early as both of us can remember, we each dreamed of seeing the glory of God. We read the Scriptures hungrily to find hope of realizing the dream of seeing His glory manifested. More maturity brought a desire to see the glory of God displayed in our lives. We recognized that our aim in life was not just to behold His glory, but to glorify Him by our every action. We simply did not want to miss out on any part of it.

Eventually we understood that the glory of God is all-inclusive of His Kingdom. Everything about God's Kingdom radiates His glory. It is reflected in His every act, and in every response from us that is prompted by His Spirit. His glory radiates from the life of God Himself and goes on to permeate all creation. Our relationship with Him is His crowning achievement, and it would take a world of books to cover the depths of the glory that will be realized in this relationship.

Now Ché Ahn has written a book that helps us both to perceive God's glory and to pursue it. By exploring the many facets of this subject, Ché has earnestly tried to leave nothing out of his book that is helpful in our quest for God's glory. We wish we had been able to read such a book when we were young. We are eagerly feeding at the feast his book provides us now.

Ché's book takes us to a broad variety of places in God's Kingdom to uncover as much of His glory as possible in one volume. To read this book is to rejoice deeply over our position and future in Christ, and to be overcome by the sheer, raw beauty of our God and all that He does around us and in us. God designed us to share in His glory, and through His Son, He has provided us with the ability to drink deeply and be satisfied. Ché's book will be used to lead many to just such refreshment.

Paging through this book, it is clear why Jesus led Ché to write it. Ché himself has, for a long time, had a deep longing to see and experience the glory of God. He hungrily pursued the Lord during his many years of pastoring, and was rewarded when renewal came from Toronto Airport Christian Fellowship to his own church, Harvest Rock in Pasadena, California. Ché saw much of the glory of God manifested when his church hosted renewal nightly for three and a half years. The supernatural was much in evidence during those years, and in experiencing it, Ché became increasingly hungry for God's glory. Both he and his wife, Sue, became carriers of God's glory, hungry hosts for His Holy Spirit, and contenders for His abiding presence on earth.

We know God is glorified when His people cry out with a united voice for righteousness and holiness in the land. Ché's quest for God's glory led to his church's involvement with The Call, a series of convocations calling the Body of Christ to fasting, repentance and prayer. Initially these gatherings were held at locations all over the United States, and now they are also being held internationally. Ché saw the Lord respond to these meetings with power and favor, as large numbers of youth were deeply challenged and repentant, wanting nothing but to see God's glory manifested in their lives. Once hunger builds for the glory of God, nothing else can replace it. Once the goodness of the Lord is tasted, there is nowhere to go but up, closer to His heart and purposes.

As a couple in ministry, we live for His presence. Our daily prayer is, "Possess me, Holy Spirit. Pick me up like a paintbrush in the Master's hand, completely yielded to You in love." This book is that kind of paintbrush, as Ché takes us with him in his quest for God's glory, relating each step in his own spiritual journey. We have tasted and enjoyed many things in our walk with Jesus, but Ché points us to the ultimate: the glory of God Himself. He shows us that not only does God glorify Himself, but as He powerfully works in us, we glorify Him and can enjoy Him forever. To have an entire book in our hands dedicated to the glory of God is exciting spiritual wealth.

This book is more than information; it is impartation. It is more than knowledge, as it offers accounts of actual encounters with the glory of God's liquid love. We encourage each reader to digest this book slowly and enjoy it thoughtfully and thoroughly. May its contents draw you up the very mountain of the Lord and reveal Christ in you as the "hope of glory," until that very glory covers the earth "as the waters cover the sea" (Habakkuk 2:14). And may God be glorified by every word and response.

—Rolland and Heidi Baker
Iris Ministries
Pemba, Mozambique

Preface

A strong cry is rising from the hearts of God's people. This cry is for the glory of God to be released on the Church in greater ways. And while reflected by songwriters and great preachers around the world, the cry has not originated from directives given by men or women of God, or even from the disciplined study of Scripture. The cry has actually been birthed in the heart of God Himself. It is His desire. He longs for His glory to rest on our gatherings, our personal lives and our cities until the entire earth is filled with His glory.

In *When Heaven Comes Down*, Ché Ahn masterfully employs three streams of inspiration that help us embrace all that God intends for us. First, he gives us strong biblical underpinnings for the glory of God in order to build our hope and fuel our hunger. His scriptural insights become the roadmap to help us pursue the "more" God has promised. Second, Ché carefully uses examples from Church history. While not equal in value to the Scriptures themselves, they provide illustrations of the kind of price our forefathers were willing to pay for the breakthroughs they enjoyed. And finally, Ché's personal experiences in the glory of God are compelling enough in themselves to cause the reader to advance greatly in a Kingdom lifestyle.

My heart burned as I read these pages. It is impossible to read this book and not pick up heaven's cry that the glory of the Lord will fill the earth.

One of the great privileges of my life is to be in a covenantal relationship with Ché Ahn. Our commitment to each other is not just because we live in the same state and share a common vision for the people we serve. It comes out of a deep appreciation in each of us for the grace and glory that rests upon the other's life.

This endorsement, then, is for the man, his message and this book. They are perfectly intertwined. *When Heaven Comes Down* is practical, educational and intensely inspirational. It comes from the rich revival heritage found in Ché's life and it is filled with encounters of God's glory. If you read it slowly and prayerfully, you will experience the heart of God for His Church in this hour.

—Bill Johnson
senior pastor, Bethel Church, Redding, Calif.
author, *When Heaven Invades Earth*
and *Face to Face with God*

Acknowledgments

I want to thank with my whole heart Linda Radford and Calista Wu. You have done a tremendous job of editing this book. Thank you for your labor of love.

I also want to thank Jane Campbell and Chosen Books for taking on this project and for publishing it. Jane, it is such a joy to work with you. Thank you for your servant's heart.

I also want to thank my family and the members of Harvest Rock Church. You consistently demonstrate a hunger for His presence and truly live for His glory. It is an honor to serve you as your pastor.

Finally, I want to thank all the churches and ministries that represent Harvest International Ministry (HIM) around the globe. You are a partial fulfillment of what was prophesied in Habakkuk 2:14: "For the earth will be filled with the knowledge of the glory of the LORD, as the waters cover the sea."

Introduction

A Visitation of Glory

My wife, Sue, had no idea what she was about to behold as she unlocked the doors of the dark and empty Mott Auditorium in the middle of the night. Our two young daughters, Joy and Mary, and their friend Christine stood by her side. As the doors opened, all of them gasped in unison as they immediately beheld an unparalleled vision of the manifest glory of heaven. Sue and the girls stood transfixed, trying to take it all in.

A white mist filled the building. Through the mist they saw thousands of translucent doves resting on the chairs and lining the rafters. Bright colors of heaven, previously unknown, flooded their eyes. The entire floor was covered in a carpet of luminous grass and laced with heavenly flowers in brilliant colors that blazed like jewels. They could hear strains of the most beautiful music and realized it was the flowers singing. Hundreds of majestic angels of every size and ethnicity were visible throughout the vast auditorium, many of them enormous, towering thirty to forty feet toward the ceiling.

It was in the early hours on a Sunday morning in May 1995, long after the Saturday evening service had ended. Our church, Harvest Rock, was barely a year old. We had earnestly sought a visitation from the Lord during that first year, and we had taken a major step of faith to rent Mott Auditorium for our meetings. At $35,000 a month, it was a great stretch for us. We had been holding meetings at the Mott building in north Pasadena almost nightly for over a month, and our congregation was experiencing wonderful times in the Lord.

Earlier on this particular Saturday night Sue and I had been tucked into bed, but I was having no success getting to sleep. Our daughter Joy and her friend Christine were camped in the living room, next to our bedroom, and we could hear their laughter, which had continued for some time. Finally I asked Sue if she would help the girls quiet down. Sleepily, she complied, crawling out of bed.

As Sue entered the living room, she realized that both girls had been overcome with holy laughter. Shaking under the power of the Holy Spirit, Christine cried out to my wife, "Mott, Mott, we've got to go to Mott!" indicating the auditorium. Joy immediately chimed in, "Yes, Mother, we've got to go to Mott!"

It was nearly one o'clock in the morning. Yet Sue sensed strongly that God was moving on the children, so she decided to take them. She loaded the two girls and our younger daughter, Mary, into the family van and drove to the auditorium.

As they stood amazed by the glorious sights surrounding them, one of the girls cried, "We have to get Pastor Lou!" Lou Engle, one of our pastors at Harvest Rock Church, lived just across the street from the auditorium. He and his wife, Therese, had chosen that location so Lou could walk to the early morning prayer meetings he led daily. Lou has a passion for intercessory prayer, and since that night, he has become president of The Call, an international movement that has mobilized massive assemblies of people who pray for revival and spiritual awakening all over the world.

Quickly crossing the street from Mott, Sue and the girls roused Lou from sleep to come and behold the glory-filled auditorium. Lou rushed back with them, and as he entered the auditorium, he felt a heaviness in the air, like a presence, but couldn't see anything. Sue and the girls, though, continued to see the vision they had gazed on earlier. Because the children were describing such spectacular things, including angels thirty to forty feet tall, Lou decided to separate Joy and Christine and interview each girl alone. Even under his detailed questioning, each child continued to describe the incredible sights and sounds in the same way. Lou was convinced the children were witnessing a heavenly visitation of the glory of God.

The next morning, I learned of the incident while on my way to the church. When I arrived, I, too, felt an increased presence of God in the building but saw nothing. Yet that night's meeting, which was conducted as usual, was clearly different. It marked the beginning of a period of angelic visitation and manifest glory in our services. For the next six months, the girls and other children continued to see angels during our meetings. It was as if heaven had descended on us.

That is what God's glory is—heaven coming to earth!

Harvest Rock Church has enjoyed seasons of heavenly visitation ever since that first manifestation of God's glory in our midst. These manifestations do not always come in the same way. There isn't always a visitation of angels, for example. Sometimes God's glory descends like a thick fog, filling the building, even though the sky outside is crystal clear. At other times we feel the glory of God as a weighty presence around us when we worship or pray. Yet whenever the glory of God comes, there is always some type of manifestation. His glory is weighty and heavy. It is real, with substance, impacting us and our surroundings. And we have discovered that His glory carries His presence, and He is more real than anything else in the universe.

In His grace, God chose to bless our church with the manifest presence of His glory. His visitation marked us as a prophetic house and a dwelling place for His Spirit. Yet, like God Himself, His glory can never be fully contained or definitively explained. But His glory can be experienced in joyful awe and wonder. And as we have experienced traces of His glory we have been left hungry for more of Him.

In my heartfelt desire to know God, I am eager to experience more of His glory. I am finding in my encounters with His glory that I become more intimately acquainted with Him. My prayer with this book is that as I share my own experiences and those of others, you too will be encouraged to pursue the glory of God.

1

What Is Glory?

A member of Harvest Rock Church shared this story with me:

A few years ago, I was desperately seeking more of God. I spent hours praying and meditating on Scripture, but I couldn't seem to get filled. I wanted, indeed, craved *more!*

I had been in my bedroom seeking God on my face for several hours when I felt a presence begin to intensify in the room. It is hard to describe, but it felt like a warmth and peace invading the atmosphere. In my spirit, I heard the Lord quietly speak: *I want to come in here with you. May I get closer?* I audibly replied, "Yes, Lord."

The presence began to intensify. A sense of weight, a kind of heaviness, began to grow. I felt the warmth begin to surge around my body, as if I were being surrounded by a whirlpool of warm energy. It was exhilarating, and for a few moments I felt incredible peace and bliss, close to ecstasy. The presence kept intensifying, and suddenly I realized I was in the grip of Someone vast, beyond my comprehension.

I was overwhelmed by it all, and I cried out, "Lord, you're frightening me." Immediately, the presence pulled back and gave me space. I sensed at once both the Lord's eagerness to be close to me and His desire to respect my limitations and not frighten me. It was a bittersweet moment, and I burst into tears as I suddenly understood how much more He longed for me than I did for Him.

This story makes me smile because it depicts a tendency we all have. We all want the Lord—until He actually shows up and we encounter His glory! Suddenly we are confronted by His reality, rather than just having knowledge about Him. At such times, all our doctrinal decrees of what God is like and how He behaves simply evaporate.

It is easy to confuse our ideas about God with God Himself. Even our ideas based on Scripture cannot contain the reality of direct exposure to God and His glory. Kris Vallotton, in his book *Developing a Supernatural Lifestyle*, puts it this way:

> Many people know the Bible and think they know the Lord. The goal of the Scriptures is to lead us into a relationship with Jesus. Having a relationship with God should never be mistaken for knowing the Scriptures. If knowing the Bible was synonymous with knowing God, the Pharisees and Scribes would have rocked![1]

If we want to know God personally and relate to Him intimately, we must be prepared to receive and experience His glory.

God and His Glory Inseparable

We simply cannot have a living encounter with God without encountering His glory. This cannot happen any more than

I can visit you and leave my body at home. Everywhere I go my body goes, because my body and I are one. The same is true for God and His glory—they are one. When God shows up, so does His glory.

As God's presence invades our surroundings, His glory enters and often manifests itself. This experience may be beautiful and inspiring, as it was for us with the angelic visitation at Mott Auditorium. Or, an experience of His glory may be overwhelming or heartrending or even mirthful. No matter what our experience, encountering His glory always impacts and changes us. It stretches our understanding of God and His ways and frequently challenges our current conceptions of Him. Although our words about God are safe and containable, God Himself is not, and this is also true of His glory. It is untamable, unpredictable, and frequently provokes controversy, especially when it violates our "norms" for God.

Just what is God's glory?

Glory Defined

Most attributes of God are far too vast to define. This applies whether we're speaking of God's mercy and love or of His righteousness and judgment. The same is true of His glory. The Bible uses words for *glory* more than 350 times, making it one of Scripture's primary themes and one with many dimensions.

To help briefly define glory, I consulted two professors at Azusa Pacific University who are members of Harvest Rock Church, the husband-wife team of Dr. Todd Pokrifka, Professor of New Testament Theology, and Dr. Junia Pokrifka, Professor of Old Testament Theology. In their thorough study of the concept of God's glory in Scripture, the Pokrifkas identified two main categories of glory: God's *eternal glory* and His *manifest glory*. Here is a summation of what they shared with me.

God's Eternal Glory and His Manifest Glory

Very few passages in the Bible speak directly of or allude to God's *eternal* glory, but many refer to His *manifest* glory. The distinction between these two categories of glory can be illustrated in terms of light. In fact, the Bible often uses the language of light to describe God's glory.

Think of the sun and the sun's light. The *eternal* glory of God is like the sun itself, far too fiery and brilliant for us to encounter directly or even to look at. But the sun's light manifests itself to us in a variety of ways. It illuminates darkness, revealing the objects around us. It gives us spectacular light displays in beautiful sunrises and brilliant sunsets. It warms us and even tans our skin. Everywhere the sun goes, the sun's light goes. But the sun's light is not the sun itself. Rather, the light we experience from the sun is a *manifestation* of the sun.

This distinction is helpful in understanding God's glory. His *eternal* glory is like the sun: it is His very essence, beyond our comprehension or ability to encounter. Yet His *manifest* glory is like the sun's light: a reflection of Him we can encounter in ways we are able to perceive, whether through physical healing, a peaceful presence in our spirit or an angelic visitation.

God's Eternal Glory in Scripture

Even before God's glory was *manifest* in creation, God had *eternal* glory. Jesus speaks of the glory He had with the Father prior to the creation of the world, a glory to which He would return after His ascension. "Now, Father, glorify me in your presence with the glory I had with you before the world began" (John 17:5).

Scripture also refers to God's *eternal* glory as the brilliant and splendid light that God is. "God is light; in him there is no darkness at all" (1 John 1:5). In heaven, no light is necessary because God Himself is the source of all light visible to His creatures, with its beautiful nature and life-giving properties.

In Scripture God's inherent, eternal glory is seen as His worthiness and importance. *Strong's Dictionary* defines *glory* as "abundance, honor, glory, riches, wealth, splendor." Likewise, the New Testament Greek word *doxa* speaks of God's glory in terms of His brightness, praise, majesty and honor.

In the Old Testament, the most frequently used word for *glory* is the Hebrew *kabôd*, a word related to the verb *kabed*, which signifies "to be heavy." Coupled with the Greek *doxa* and *Strong's* definition, *kabôd* rounds out God's glory as having weightiness and importance as well as value and worth.

In every sense of these definitions, Jesus Christ shares the same eternal glory and honor as God the Father: "Jesus Christ. To him be the glory and the power for ever and ever" (1 Peter 4:11).

God's Manifest Glory in Scripture

The *manifest* glory of God is God revealing Himself, in His eternal glory, in and through creation and people. Most references to God's glory in Scripture are descriptions of His manifest glory. And God manifests His glory to us in many ways.

When God created the world, He revealed His glory in and through what He made. Simply put, creation is an expression of God's manifest glory. The heavens lead all of creation in declaring the glory of God and in revealing the magnificent power, creativity and intelligence of God the Creator. "The heavens declare the glory of God; the skies proclaim the work of his hands" (Psalm 19:1). This glory remains evident even after the fall of humankind into sin and the subsequent corruption of creation.

Because humankind was created in God's image and likeness, human beings express the glory of God in a special way. "A man ought not to cover his head, since he is the image and glory of God" (1 Corinthians 11:7). Indeed, humankind was created to glorify God. The glory we're given is a "derived glory," which comes from our union with God through our obedience to Him and through our being filled with God's Spirit.

From the very beginning, God intended that humankind would know Him through His glory, as expressed in His manifest presence, His manifest nature and character and His manifest power. For this reason, God's *manifest glory* is the major focus of this book.

A Working Definition of God's Glory

God's glory is far too vast and complex to comprehend, let alone ever to define perfectly. But to allow for clear communication in this book, I would like to propose this working definition:

> God's glory is His manifest presence, by which He reveals His character of goodness and displays His power through signs and wonders.

Throughout Scripture, God calls His people to know Him, to glorify Him and to reflect His glory. To truly know God, we must encounter His glory. And the more intimately we know God, the more His glory will be revealed to us and in us.

In the next few chapters, we will delve more deeply into the different facets of God's *manifest* glory and explore the effects this glory has on our lives. We will examine (1) His manifest presence, (2) His manifest nature and character and (3) His manifest power. We'll look at examples of these in the Bible, throughout church history and in present-day encounters that people have had with His glory.

We also will consider what we need to do to stay in the flow of God's glory, going from glory to glory. Finally, we will conclude with the purpose of God's glory, which is the transformation of ourselves and society, so that the prayer Jesus taught us will be answered: "Your kingdom come, your will be done on earth as it is in heaven" (Matthew 6:10).

2

Glory as the Manifest Presence of God

And it came to pass, when Moses entered the tabernacle, that the pillar of cloud descended and stood at the door of the tabernacle, and the LORD talked with Moses. All the people saw the pillar of cloud standing at the tabernacle door, and all the people rose and worshiped, each man in his tent door.

Exodus 33:9–10, NKJV

While Aaron was speaking to the whole Israelite community, they looked toward the desert, and there was the glory of the LORD appearing in the cloud.

Exodus 16:10

Then the cloud covered the Tent of Meeting, and the glory of the LORD filled the tabernacle. Moses could not enter the Tent of Meeting because the cloud had settled upon it, and the glory of the LORD filled the tabernacle.

Exodus 40:34–35

Most of us are familiar with the account of Moses and the Israelites following God's leading through the wilderness. They were able to follow Him because He manifested His glory to them in the form of a cloud. Even those who have never read this account in Scripture have probably seen it depicted in the classic Cecil B. DeMille movie, *The Ten Commandments.*

We may think of the passages above as God's special appearances to Moses and Israel while they were in the wilderness. But God's glory has appeared many times and in many different forms to His people.

God Visits His People

We see how God visited His people hundreds of years after the wilderness experience, during King Solomon's reign. King Solomon had completed the Temple and was bringing the Ark of the Covenant to its new home. There was a solemn procession into the Temple and the Ark was placed in the holy of holies. The priests withdrew, and outside the singers and musicians began to praise God.

Scripture then tells us:

> The trumpeters and singers joined in unison, as with one voice, to give praise and thanks to the LORD. Accompanied by trumpets, cymbals and other instruments, they raised their voices in praise to the LORD and sang: "He is good; his love endures forever." Then the temple of the LORD was filled with a cloud, and the priests could not perform their service because of the cloud, for the glory of the LORD filled the temple of God.
>
> 2 Chronicles 5:13–14

This passage makes clear that wherever God is present His glory is present also, for God and His glory are one. They cannot be separated and I will refer to God's glory and His presence interchangeably throughout this book. One aspect of God's glory is that it is the luminous manifest presence of His person. This manifest presence is the power and presence of the Holy Spirit displaying His glory in a tangible way. It is as if a curtain is pulled back and people are allowed to experience heaven invading earth.

God's Presence Manifests in Many Forms

The examples from the Bible I have provided above all refer to God's glorious manifest presence as a cloud. But, of course, His glory isn't limited to one form of tangible expression. Let's look at some other manifestations of the glory of His presence, as provided in Scripture.

Fire

The angel of the LORD appeared to (Moses) in flames of fire within a bush. Moses saw that though the bush was on fire it did not burn up. . . . When the LORD saw that (Moses) had gone over to look, God called to him from within the bush, "Moses! Moses!" . . . "Do not come any closer," God said. "Take off your sandals, for the place where you are standing is holy ground."

Exodus 3:2, 4–5

When Solomon finished praying, fire came down from heaven and consumed the burnt offering and the sacrifices, and the glory of the LORD filled the temple. The priests could not enter the temple of the LORD because the glory of the LORD filled it.

2 Chronicles 7:1–2

When the day of Pentecost came, they were all together in one place. . . . They saw what seemed to be tongues of fire that separated and came to rest on each of them. All of them were filled with the Holy Spirit and began to speak in other tongues as the Spirit enabled them.

Acts 2:1, 3–4

Brilliant Light

As (Saul) neared Damascus on his journey, suddenly a light from heaven flashed around him. He fell to the ground and heard a voice say to him, "Saul, Saul, why do you persecute me?" "Who are you, Lord?" Saul asked. "I am Jesus, whom you are persecuting," he replied.

Acts 9:3–5

After six days Jesus took Peter, James and John with him and led them up a high mountain, where they were all alone. There he was transfigured before them. His clothes became dazzling white, whiter than anyone in the world could bleach them. And there appeared before them Elijah and Moses, who were talking with Jesus.

Mark 9:2–4

When I [John] turned I saw seven golden lampstands, and among the lampstands was someone "like a son of man," dressed in a robe reaching down to his feet and with a golden sash around his chest. . . . His face was like the sun shining in all its brilliance.

Revelation 1:12–13, 16

Sound

On the morning of the third day there was thunder and lightning, with a thick cloud over the mountain, and a very loud trumpet blast. Everyone in the camp trembled. Then Moses led the people out of the camp to meet with God, and they stood at the foot of the mountain.

Exodus 19:16–17

As soon as Jesus was baptized, he went up out of the water
... and a voice from heaven said, "This is my Son, whom I
love; with him I am well pleased."

Matthew 3:16, 17

When the day of Pentecost came, they were all together in
one place. Suddenly a sound like the blowing of a violent
wind came from heaven and filled the whole house where
they were sitting.

Acts 2:1–2

These are just a few examples of the many forms that the
glory of God's manifest presence may take. We're comfort-
able reading about these accounts because, as dramatic as
they are, we know they all happened a long time ago. Yet
imagine the effect if you were to witness them taking place
today.

Does God still tangibly manifest the glory of His presence
today? The answer is yes!

God's Presence Is within Us and Also Comes to Us

Some Christians believe that since the Spirit of God dwells
within us, there is no need for God to manifest His presence
to us. After all, we have His presence with us at all times,
everywhere we go.

It is true that if you have been a Christian for any length of
time, you have probably learned ways to sense the presence
of the Holy Spirit within you. Perhaps you sometimes hear
a still, small voice within you giving you guidance. At other
times you may feel a deep sense of quiet contentment as you
experience the peace of God's presence. Or, you may feel
energized as a passage of Scripture suddenly comes alive to
you, with God's Spirit giving you divine insight.

Yet even though God's presence is *within us*, His presence can also *come to us*. At such times we may powerfully experience Him in tangible ways. You see, our God is extravagant and loves to make Himself known to us in a variety of ways. He loves for us to seek Him and to entreat Him to come to us. And when we do so, seeking His presence—whether individually or corporately, through praise, worship, prayer, meditation or simply quieting ourselves and waiting upon Him—He comes to us. And the more earnestly and persistently we seek Him, the more He manifests the glory of His presence to us. To know God intimately is to experience His glory, and we need to expect that sometimes the experience will be a tangible one.

What I am describing is all part of the Kingdom-restoration work God is doing through His Son, Jesus Christ. God's purpose is to restore us to the abundance and fullness of life He originally created us for, including our relationship of communion with Him. The Bible tells us that in Eden the Lord walked and talked with Adam and Eve in the cool of the day (see Genesis 3:8). I don't believe Adam and Eve walked and talked with a still, small, inner voice. I believe they walked and talked with a tangible presence, the manifest presence of God Himself. And that is part of the restoration He intends for us: We are reconciled to Father God, not only through His abolishing of the spiritual barrier of sin, but also in His invitation for us to come into the glory of His literal, tangible presence.

Present-Day Manifestations of God's Presence

A member of Harvest Rock Church shares her experience with God's manifest presence:

> I remember the first time I saw the *shekinah* [glory] of God's presence. I had been baptized in the Spirit only two weeks and had never read or heard about the *shekinah*.

We were visiting a church that was very active in the charismatic movement. It was very crowded when we arrived, so we were seated in back of the podium facing the congregation. As I sat there, I began to feel a heavy presence, like a blanket of warmth and peace settling over me. Then I saw "it." It was near the ceiling, over the people's heads at the back of the sanctuary. It looked like a fog and began rolling forward. At first I thought someone must have opened the outside doors at the back of the building and fog must be coming in from outside.

But I realized that couldn't be the explanation. This was Houston, Texas, in the middle of summer. There was no fog outside! Besides, as this unusual "inside fog" kept rolling forward, it grew thicker and didn't look like ordinary fog. It glistened as if it had flecks of gold in it. The best way to describe it was "a golden mist." It just kept rolling forward, and the heavy presence kept intensifying. It was clearly visible to me, but as I glanced around, no one else seemed to be noticing it. I knew it had to be from God, but I had no idea what it was.

Several weeks later, back in my home church, we were studying the dedication of Solomon's Temple and how the glory cloud of the Lord filled the Temple. Suddenly, I knew what I had seen, and I thanked the Lord.

I smiled as I heard this member's story, because it so paralleled my own first experience with God's glory cloud. In the midst of that experience, my rational mind kicked in and I tried to make sense of what I was seeing. Yet I knew it couldn't be ordinary fog, as it wasn't foggy outside. So I started praising God as the heavenly fog thickened, until I could scarcely see anyone in front of me. It was pure glory!

Some people have "open visions" of God's glory, in which they see into the heavenly realm, as did my wife and the girls at Mott. They behold all sorts of beautiful things like angels, flowers, strange creatures, lovely meadows, and trees laden with fruit. Sometimes with an open vision, they also receive a word of prophecy, or hear glorious music or choirs of angels singing. Regardless of what they see or hear, they all report the unmistakable sense of being in the presence of God.

While at a conference in Las Vegas, a member of our church experienced another type of manifestation of God's presence. At the end of a particular session, the speakers asked the people to come forward so they could lay hands on them for an impartation of God's Spirit. During the procession, the assembly sang the chorus "Let It Rain," and soon people felt water droplets falling from the ceiling. As they looked up, it appeared to be *raining indoors*. They knew the roof couldn't be leaking because it was sunny outside. Someone thought the air conditioning might be leaking, so he informed the management, but technicians could find no problem with the air conditioning system.

The water droplets kept falling lightly, and suddenly our church member realized what was happening. The gathering had been singing "Let It Rain," asking God to open the windows of heaven and pour His glory upon them—and He was doing just that. I personally believe He was giving us all a prophetic sign in those water droplets, indicating He is about to drench the world with a fresh outpouring of His glory!

Fortunately, our member was able to locate a camera and film the indoor rain coming down. She brought it back to Harvest Rock and showed it to our congregation. Needless to say, we were excited and blessed!

One of the more unique manifestations of God's presence I've heard about was related to me by a fellow pastor who had attended services led by Kathryn Kuhlman in the 1970s. At one service Miss Kuhlman invited a couple from a foreign country to approach the platform, saying to them, "Come up here. The Lord has something for you."

As they walked up the center aisle toward the platform, a powerful wind blew against them, hindering their progress.

They both had to lean forward to keep from falling as they walked into the wind. The couple's clothes flapped wildly as the people around them gazed on in wonder.

My pastor friend said he looked around to find the source of the wind but saw no fans or anything else that might be causing it. Stranger still, the wind blew only along the center aisle. Everywhere else in the auditorium the air was perfectly still. Miss Kuhlman laughed when she saw the couple struggling and told them, "Don't be afraid, dear ones, that's the wind of the Holy Spirit blowing on you."

Bodily Manifestations of God's Presence

Not all manifestations of God's presence involve seeing or hearing heavenly things. When God's presence fills a place, people often experience physical sensations and have bodily reactions. Some of these are reactions that many Christians can identify with. Examples of this are feeling "caught up" in joy or peace while worshiping, or losing track of time while in prayer or meditation.

But sometimes God's presence is intense, and so are people's bodily responses. His presence may bring joy and laughter— gut-wrenching, side-splitting, rolling-on-the-floor laughter. Sometimes people's bodies jerk uncontrollably as if they're getting an electric shock. People may bob and weave rhythmically or shake with tremors. At times people fall over and remain on the floor. It is not uncommon for these people to report feeling temporarily immobilized or even stuck to the floor. I know of a few cases where others tried to help them get up but couldn't because the glory of the Lord was so heavy upon them.

Often people report feeling waves of warmth or even currents of power going through them. In response they may laugh, cry, grunt, groan, scream, sing, speak in tongues or become very still and quiet, seemingly lost in God's presence. The first time I experienced anything like this was as a junior in high school, during a youth choir trip with a friend's church. I had been a Christian for just over a year and was eager to know God more deeply. Our choir was performing during an evening service, and we began singing a song I liked very much.

I was particularly stirred that night, and I sang from deep within my heart. I felt as if the song had become my prayer. Suddenly, my hands started to tingle intensely, and I realized I couldn't move them. The tingling quickly moved up my arms and began surging throughout my body. Before I knew it, I began sobbing and I couldn't stop.

The youth director approached me and gently suggested I leave the platform. Unable to do anything but cry, I somehow managed to stumble into the men's room, where I continued to sob for some time. God's presence was so real and strong on me that I automatically responded with body-racking sobs and a heart overflowing with joy. The Lord was giving me a beautiful gift in that men's room. He was baptizing me in His Spirit.

Biblical Precedents for Bodily Responses to God's Manifest Presence

As you might imagine, when you walk into a corporate setting where the glory of God's presence is manifesting, the scene might appear a little chaotic. Some people may be laughing, others crying or groaning, others jerking or twitching, while some remain very still. Yet to judge these things by outward appearances alone can be misleading. Indeed, it has led to much criticism from certain church groups. They express concern that people are being swept up into excessive behaviors and displays of mere emotionalism. They feel certain that these types of actions would never be from God.

They forget what happened on the Day of Pentecost. God visited and filled the 120 disciples gathered in the Upper Room with the Holy Spirit. These people behaved so strangely that passersby mistook them for being drunk. Peter had to give an explanation to the public, saying, "These people are not drunk as you suppose."

Have you ever seen a group of drunks together? What do they look like? Some laugh; some cry. Most have difficulty standing or walking and weave, jerk or bob instead. Some yell, some sing and some just sit, appearing to be "out of it." We can assume that at least some of these behaviors occurred at Pentecost because onlookers thought the disciples were drunk.

And what about those people who fall down in the Spirit and lie motionless on the ground? We have the account of a credible, firsthand witness that this is a legitimate response to the Lord's manifest presence. Writing from the isle of Patmos, the apostle John states, "When I saw him [Jesus], I fell at his feet as though dead" (Revelation 1:17).

To anyone who has concerns about whether these things can be of God, I invite you to look again, this time with the eyes of your heart. Our Father God is so loving and knows us so well that when His presence enters and touches us, He ministers to us in ways we most need and can receive at that moment. For some weighed down by sadness or worry, a refreshing session of holy laughter is just what they need, as God reminds them they can relinquish their burdens to Him. For others, a time of sobbing may allow them to release some deep pain and wounds as they find themselves wrapped in the comforting arms of the Holy Spirit. Still others may find themselves entering into someone else's sorrow or pain while interceding for them, as the Lord shares His own burden for them. And some people just want to bask in God's presence and gaze upon His loveliness.

I realize that the subject of manifestations is new and controversial for many Christians. John Arnott, pastor of the Toronto Airport Christian Fellowship, hosted a revival known as the "Toronto Blessing" for over twelve years, and it was characterized by many types of physical manifestations of God's presence. He has written two books, *The Father's Blessing* and *Experience the Blessing: Testimonies from Toronto*, which contain descriptions and scriptural explanations of these types of phenomena. I heartily recommend these books to readers who want to pursue more in-depth information in this area.[1]

One thing I do know for sure, for I have seen it time and time again. Everyone who encounters the presence of God regardless of manifestations that occur, leaves refreshed, strengthened, encouraged, often significantly changed and always reassured of God's love for them.

Presence with a Purpose

At Harvest Rock Church, we welcome the presence of God in every one of our meetings. We expect Him to show up, and we never try to second-guess what He is going to do. We want to be touched by the glory of His presence, for it infuses us with a renewed sense of who we are as His children.

We have learned through our experiences that God is not an absent parent. He likes frequent and intimate contact with His children. Often in His presence, we His children receive prophetic insight about His calling for our lives, or experience deep inner healing setting us free. He also reveals to us mysteries of His plan and purpose, and we always leave feeling we know Him more deeply.

Finally, we have learned that God is not predictable, yet that keeps our journey with Him fresh and exciting. As one of the children in *The Chronicles of Narnia* book series says of the Christ figure Aslan, "He's a good lion, but not a tame one." We understand that these encounters with God's presence are maturing us, molding and shaping us into the image of Christ. And we know that as we grow individually and corporately, He is restoring us to abundant life and equipping us to perform His heart's desire.

God wants us to usher in His Kingdom on earth by transforming the world around us. We will be taking a deeper look at His glory and the fulfillment of His purpose in us throughout the rest of this book.

3

Glory as the Revealed Goodness of God

As a minister's son, I spent my early years sitting in church and listening to sermons about Jesus. But by the time I was a teenager, I was leading a life filled with drugs, alcohol and parties. On the outside my life may have looked exciting and fun, but inside I felt empty and frustrated.

One night when I was seventeen, I went to a party at a friend's house, where I got loaded on beer and pot. Hours later, I found myself bored with the party atmosphere. I felt strangely alone and empty and wandered into a vacant bedroom, where I closed the door behind me. Feeling overwhelmed, I heard myself cry out to God.

"Lord," I prayed, "I don't know if You exist. But if You do, and if what my parents told me as a boy is true—that You died for my sins and there is a heaven and a hell—I want You to reveal Yourself to me. I want You to reveal the truth to me."

At that moment, I felt a surge of warmth and love surrounding my body, a sensation unlike any I had ever experienced. My mind suddenly was clear, and I knew that Jesus was real. I was so overwhelmed with how much He loved me that I began to weep uncontrollably. Filled with this revelation of Jesus, I couldn't contain my joy. I immediately ran to tell my friends.

"Guys, I found what we're all looking for," I declared. "It's Jesus! Jesus just revealed Himself to me tonight." My friends looked at me as if I had taken one toke too many of the pot. "Don't worry, Ché," they told me, "you'll be all right in the morning."

But for the next three days I could not stop weeping, as waves of God's love washed over me. Two weeks later I made a quality decision to surrender my life to Jesus, and I was set free from drugs and my lifestyle.

When I gave God the opportunity to reveal Himself, He manifested His presence, immersing me in a profound experience of His love, joy, mercy and goodness. From that moment on, my life has never been the same.

Show Me Your Glory

The glory of God reveals His core nature and character, which includes His goodness, kindness, love and compassion. We are given a revelation of this as we examine God's amazing interaction with Moses.

The Bible tells us that Moses was close to God, sharing with Him a unique bond unparalleled by anyone else at the time. During Israel's journey in the wilderness, Moses met with God in the Tabernacle. According to Scripture, their intimacy was such that God talked to Moses as one would talk to a friend. Yet, though his relationship with God far surpassed that of others, Moses was still hungry for the Lord, wanting more of Him. So he made this audacious request of God: "Now show me your glory" (Exodus 33:18).

The Lord replied, "I will cause all my goodness to pass in front of you, and I will proclaim my name, the LORD, in your presence. I will have mercy on whom I will have mercy, and I will have compassion on whom I will have compassion" (Exodus 33:19).

God could have said, "I will let my justice pass in front of you," or, "I will let my omnipotence pass in front of you." Instead, the Lord specifically said, "I will cause all my goodness to pass in front of you." The part of His character that God wanted most to reveal to Moses was His goodness. He wanted His servant to know, above all else, that He desired to pour out His goodness upon him and Israel.

When God's glory comes, all of His goodness comes. And when His goodness comes, there is mercy, compassion, love and healing. Our God is a good God.

Show Me Your Goodness

Jesus Christ: The Embodiment of God's Goodness

Nowhere in all of God's encounters with man does He make His goodness more clearly visible than in the life and ministry of Jesus Christ. Jesus is the ultimate manifestation of the glory of God's goodness.

> The Word [Jesus] became human and made His home among us. He was full of unfailing love and faithfulness. And we have seen his glory, the glory of the Father's one and only Son. . . . No one has ever seen God. But the unique One, who is himself God, is near to the Father's heart. He has revealed God to us.
>
> John 1:14, 18, NLT

47

When we read of Jesus' actions, we see God's intentions for us demonstrated. Jesus described His own ministry by quoting the prophet Isaiah:

> The scroll of the prophet Isaiah was handed to him. Unrolling it, he found the place where it is written: "The Spirit of the Lord is on me, because he has anointed me to preach good news to the poor. He has sent me to proclaim freedom for the prisoners and recovery of sight for the blind, to release the oppressed, to proclaim the year of the Lord's favor."
>
> Luke 4:17–19

Everywhere Jesus went, He healed people, assured them they were forgiven and told them of the Father's loving concern for them. He raised the dead, stilled storms and multiplied food to feed hungry crowds. Scripture repeatedly says that Jesus looked upon people and had compassion on them. He rejected no one who sincerely sought Him, regardless of what they might have done in the past.

The apostle Peter said of Jesus, "God anointed Jesus of Nazareth with the Holy Spirit and with power, who went around doing good and healing all who were oppressed by the devil, for God was with Him" (Acts 10:38, NKJV). If we want to understand God's goodness, we need only to look at Jesus. His life, sacrificial death for us and resurrection to free us from sin and death are proof that God truly is good to us.

God Is a Good God

My family and I have experienced God's goodness in many ways over the years. A powerful demonstration of His goodness occurred when our daughter was in a major car accident. The car was so severely smashed that it had the appearance of a metal accordion, yet our daughter walked away without a scratch. When my wife and I saw the car, we burst into

48

tears at how God's goodness and mercy were manifested in protecting our child.

God longs to reveal His nature to us and to bring His goodness into our lives. But some of us are unable to recognize His goodness or fully understand it when it comes. Perhaps we have suffered a deep tragedy, and in our despair, we feel alone and abandoned by God. We may be angry or indignant toward God, wondering why He would allow something so hurtful and damaging to happen to us.

We need to realize God is not the one causing our tragedy, pain or illness. The apostle Paul explains to us, "Don't be misled, my dear brothers and sisters. Whatever is good and perfect comes down to us from God our Father, who created all the lights in the heavens. He never changes or casts a shifting shadow" (James 1:16–17, NLT).

The Lord's intentions and actions toward us are good. But we have an enemy who is malicious and merciless, wanting us to feel hopeless and betrayed by God. Satan attacks us with doubts about God's love, wanting us to believe our suffering has come from Him. But Jesus contrasted His own intentions and actions toward us with those of Satan. He said, "The thief comes only to steal and kill and destroy; I have come that they may have life, and have it to the full" (John 10:10). We can be assured that whatever brings abundant life to us is from God, and everything else is from another source.

Yet it is possible for us to know that God is good and still get discouraged at times. We may pray for change to occur in a certain situation, yet nothing seems to happen. As we wait for it to be fulfilled, we grow weary or even doubtful and may conclude that our prayer is unanswered. At such times, we may feel that God is distant and untouched by our needs. Yet nothing could be further from the truth. The author of Hebrews tells us that Jesus, having shared our humanity, is moved by our difficulties and understands our weaknesses and infirmities (see Hebrews 2:14). Moreover, Jesus personally takes our prayers to the Father by interceding for us (see Hebrews 7:25).

Often, a long-awaited answer to prayer will yield a much greater result than anything we might have expected. Just as we are to stand in faith for our salvation—a faith that is unseen yet real—we must make a choice to stand on the promise that God's nature cannot be anything except good. Perhaps you are going through a particularly hard time right now, needing a financial breakthrough, a physical healing or restoration of a relationship. I encourage you to persevere in faith. God promises breakthrough. "Weeping may endure for a night, but joy comes in the morning" (Psalm 30:5, NKJV).

A Season for Breakthrough

I personally experienced this profound truth as a young Christian. In the early years of our marriage, Sue and I were at a Billy Graham movie, munching on some popcorn, when my jaw suddenly popped and I felt a sharp pain. I realized my jaw had locked and would open only about an inch. I excused myself to the restroom, where I tried to unlock my jaw to no avail. That night before going to bed, Sue and I prayed for my healing. I was confident God would answer our prayer, because I had asked Him for personal healing before and had received it. Also, I had worked in a healing room with a local ministry and seen others receive miraculous healings. When I woke the next morning, however, my jaw was still painfully locked.

Undaunted, I continued to pray daily. After a week of no change, I made an appointment to see my brother-in-law, who is an Ear, Nose and Throat surgeon. He immediately diagnosed the problem as TMJ (temporomandibular joint disorder). When I asked what I could do to get rid of it, he informed me there was no effective treatment. Surgery might be a last resort, but I would have to learn to live with it. I went home discouraged and somewhat confused. I knew God is a healer—so why wasn't I getting healed? I certainly didn't want to spend the rest of my life eating soft food, as one of my favorite dishes is a good steak!

For a few days I was tempted to pity myself and complain to God. Instead, I spent time soaking in His presence and reading the gospel accounts of Jesus healing people. During that period of prayer and Scripture reading, there rose from deep within me an absolute certainty that the healing was mine. I determined that each time I looked in a mirror at my painfully locked jaw, I would praise God and thank Him for healing me.

I did this numerous times a day for the next eighteen months. One morning as I woke, I yawned and realized to my surprise that my mouth had easily opened to full extension. I was healed in that moment. The TMJ has never returned.

I don't know why the answer to my prayer took so long. The important matter is that I chose to trust God's goodness and believe His promises about healing. Even when nothing changed, I persisted. At times I grew discouraged and wanted to give up, but I never did.

No matter what you are facing, I encourage you to choose to believe in God's goodness. He is faithful and true to His word. You can trust Him in everything, knowing He will work it out for your good (see Romans 8:28). In his letter to the Galatians, the apostle Paul encourages us all, "Those who live to please the Spirit will harvest everlasting life from the Spirit. So let's not get tired of doing what is good. At just the right time we will reap a harvest of blessing if we don't give up" (Galatians 6:8–9, NLT).

The Many Disguises of God's Goodness

Often our ideas about what is good for us can blind us to the greater good God wants to bestow. Sometimes His goodness is already present in our lives, but we may not have a revelation of this goodness until later. Consider the account of the missionary David Livingstone, as told by Pastors Robert Lewis and Wayne Cordeiro, who spoke at a conference held by our church:

> Livingstone was one of the great missionaries to Africa. When we were sightseeing in London, we had the opportunity to visit Westminster Abbey, where Livingstone was buried. Although his body was buried in England, his heart was buried in Central Africa.
>
> When he first arrived in Africa in 1840, he found himself in a large territory overseen by a tribal chief. He had to make an alliance with this chief in order to have access to the region. Without such an alliance he might be killed at any time. So he agreed to meet with the chief.
>
> According to tradition, Livingstone learned that the chief could ask for anything that belonged to him. So Livingstone laid out everything he owned—his clothes, his books, his watch and even his goat that provided him with goat milk for his stomach ailment. Out of all the things Livingstone laid before him, the chief chose the goat. In return, he gave Livingstone his walking stick.
>
> Livingstone left the meeting very frustrated. He began to complain to God, "God, this doesn't seem fair! I needed that goat for my stomach. I would gladly have given him anything else. And all I got in exchange was this stick."
>
> Here was Livingstone in a foreign country, and the one thing that he most needed was taken from him. At that moment it was hard to believe that any good could possibly come out of the exchange. Why in the world had God let this happen?
>
> What Livingstone later discovered was that the chief had actually given Livingstone his scepter. That scepter opened the door for Livingstone to go into every single village welcomed and protected. Because of the exchange, he was able to share the gospel in Africa until the day he died.[1]

What an amazing testimony of the goodness of God. Like Livingstone, many of us have been given scepters that we see only as walking sticks. It takes revelation to be able to see the goodness of God in our lives, which is actually all around us. Instead of focusing on our "goat"—what we have lost, what has been taken from us or what we need—let us believe in the goodness of God and trust that He works for the good of those who love Him. As we do this, we will see the goodness of God unfold in our lives, as David Livingstone did. I have experienced this firsthand. From the moment God first revealed the glory of His character to me at age seventeen up to this very day, I have experienced wave after wave of His goodness in my life.

Goodness Revealed

On January 20, 1994, God poured out His Spirit in Toronto, Canada, in spectacular fashion. The Toronto Airport Christian Fellowship Church became the center of a worldwide revival, with over four million people visiting the church during the next twelve years. I flew there in October 1994 with the intention of experiencing His glory. Earlier that year I had attended a Vineyard conference, where I experienced the glory of God powerfully touching my body, knocking me over and shaking me. I had also experienced gales of holy laughter, so intense I was sure my sides would split. Those experiences were exhilarating and life-changing, and I went to Toronto expecting more of the same.

But God had a different manifestation of His glory for me in Toronto, one I never could have anticipated. While I was lying quietly on the floor in the church under the power of the Spirit, God revealed to me that I still had bitter roots in my heart related to wounds I carried from my relationship with my father. As a young child, I had been hurt by the rejection I felt when my father physically punished me for my behavior or for unsatisfactory grades at school. Without realizing it,

I carried this sense of rejection into my other relationships, negatively impacting them.

That night in Toronto, God supernaturally healed those wounds in my heart. My relationship with my father was transformed, as God opened the door for us to openly discuss the past and fully reconcile in November 1996. My dad and I now have a wonderful, open, loving relationship. I have the utmost respect for him, and I am grateful for all the sacrifices he made for his family as a father and a pastor. Because of God's goodness, I am now able to have the relationship with my father that I have always desired. Scripture tells us that this type of healing is God's will for our lives. "He will turn the hearts of the fathers to their children, and the hearts of the children to their fathers" (Malachi 4:6).

God, in all His goodness, also restored my marriage with Sue. Because I had judged my parents for rejecting me, I had similarly and unknowingly rejected Sue, unintentionally causing her great pain in our relationship. The Bible warns against doing this very thing: "Do not judge, or you too will be judged. For in the same way you judge others, you will be judged, and with the measure you use, it will be measured to you" (Matthew 7:1–2). Because I sowed discord and rejection in our marriage, Sue was hurt and began to reject me in return.

On the day my father asked me to forgive him, God brought tremendous healing into my heart and broke a spirit of rejection over my life. As a result of this reconciliation, I was able to release the same love and acceptance to Sue. God has renewed our marriage according to His goodness, and now our marriage has never been better. Our love for God and for each other deepens every day.

The Greatest Gift

My life has been a testament to God's goodness, and I give Him praise and glory for every blessing the Lord has given me. Yet the greatest gift God has given me is the unending gift of His goodness through the person of Jesus Christ. Jesus is God's goodness to us manifest in human form.

My prayer for you is the prayer of Paul in Ephesians:

> I keep asking that the God of our Lord Jesus Christ, the glorious Father, may give you the Spirit of wisdom and revelation, so that you may know him better. I pray also that the eyes of your heart may be enlightened in order that you may know the hope to which he has called you, the riches of his glorious inheritance in the saints, and his incomparably great power for us who believe.
>
> Ephesians 1:17–19

By receiving Jesus Christ, we receive the greatest gift God could ever give to man. We not only receive eternal life, we also become sons and daughters of the living God. Jesus paid the price of our sins through His death on the cross, so that we may have access to God the Father and to eternal life in heaven. Yet this access is meant for us not just after we die but in this life as well. The Bible states, "God raised us up with Christ and seated us with him in the heavenly realms in Christ Jesus" (Ephesians 2:6). This means that as children of God we have access to the heavenly realms and to God's glory now. We have been given the ability to call His goodness in heaven down to earth.

You, too, can experience God's glory, not only in eternity, but also here on earth. All of the goodness I have experienced in my life is available to you, through Christ in you, the hope of glory. Receiving Jesus Christ and standing upon the promises of His nature releases His glory—including all of His goodness—into our lives.

If you have never made a decision to receive Jesus Christ, I'd like to invite you to do so now. God wants to release the glory of His goodness upon you, but you must respond to

His invitation of love. It is very simple to do. You can simply pray this short prayer:

> Jesus, thank You that You died for my sins and rose from the dead on the third day. Jesus, I know that I have not been a perfect person, and I thank You for forgiving me of my sins and selfishness. I give You my whole heart and ask You to be Lord of my life. With Your help, I will follow You and trust You all the days of my life. Thank You for releasing Your goodness into my life. In Jesus' name, Amen.

4

Glory as the Resurrection Power of God

My first dramatic experience with God's glory in the form of His resurrection power took place when I was just a young believer, only nineteen years old. I was on my way to the Pittsburgh Charismatic Conference, accompanying an elderly pastor who drove us along the Pennsylvania Turnpike. At one point, we noticed a major accident had taken place on the other side of the freeway. A man had jumped from the overpass and onto the freeway to commit suicide.

The pastor pulled the car to the roadside. Some people were at the scene, but there was no ambulance or police car nearby. The pastor asked me to approach the scene to check whether anyone had called 911.

Crossing the freeway, I saw a person near the accident scene directing traffic with flares. I asked him, "Is that man who jumped dead?"

"Yes," he answered. My first inclination was to turn back right away to tell the pastor that the man was dead, but I felt a strong prompting to continue my inquiry.

I approached another person who was also directing traffic. "Is that man dead?" I asked.

The traffic director explained, "A nurse stopped to help. She picked up a faint pulse in him. An ambulance is on the way now."

Ready to give that report to the pastor, I turned to go back to the car. Then I heard the Holy Spirit tell me, "Pray for that body."

Already a crowd was huddling around the body. I was a new believer, and I was gripped by fear because I didn't know how to approach the situation. I certainly didn't want to make a scene.

But I knew I had to obey the Holy Spirit. As I looked at the man's broken form, it was the most appalling thing I had ever seen. There was blood and urine everywhere, and I was surprised that even a faint pulse could remain in such a damaged body. No one wanted to touch him because no one wanted to be held liable in any way. But because the Lord had told me to lay hands on the man, I said to the onlookers, "Excuse me," slipped between them and knelt beside the man. I began to pray quietly in tongues.

While in prayer, I heard the Lord ask me, "How will I receive glory in this situation unless you pray in English?" It dawned on me that because I was a Korean-American, the people around me might assume that I was speaking in Korean.

I shifted and began to pray in English. The prayer I said was simple and evangelistic: "Lord, You are a God who loves people. You died for our sins. I pray that You would reveal Your power by raising this man in Jesus' name."

The moment I finished, the man regained consciousness, turned his head and looked at me. The whole group gasped aloud. They saw the man's direct response, from unconsciousness to consciousness, after my prayer. Soon afterward the ambulance arrived.

That was the closest to the raising of a dead person I have ever personally witnessed. Here was a man with a faint pulse, close to death, who regained consciousness by the power of the Holy Spirit. It was my first lesson in knowing there is a resurrection power that brings both salvation and abundant life—and it is available to us because of what Christ accomplished at the cross.

The Power within Us

We have already defined God's glory as His manifest presence. It reveals His goodness or displays His power through signs, wonders and miracles. When God's glory is revealed, His power is often demonstrated in a variety of ways. It may split the Red Sea, quiet a storm, engrave laws on stone or multiply food to feed multitudes.

In this chapter I want to focus on God's mighty resurrection power, which can heal the sick and even raise the dead. This power is available to believers, but a large segment of the church is not aware of its reality or of their access to it. It is important we understand this power, for the Lord has commanded us to use it.

In Matthew 10:7–8, we read how Jesus sent out his disciples for hands-on training in the world around them. He instructed them, "As you go, preach this message: 'The kingdom of heaven is near.' Heal the sick, raise the dead, cleanse those who have leprosy, drive out demons. Freely you have received, freely give."

We might be tempted to think these instructions were given to the disciples only for that particular time, but Jesus gave a similar command to His disciples before He ascended into heaven. He instructed, "Go into all the world and preach the good news to all creation. . . . And these signs will accompany those who believe: In my name they will drive out demons; they will speak in new tongues; they will pick up snakes with their hands; and when they drink deadly poison, it will not hurt them at all; they will place their hands on sick people, and they will get well" (Mark 16:15, 17–18).

Note the similar commands in both passages. We are to preach the Gospel, and our declaration of the "good news" is to be accompanied by displays of God's power in healing the sick and raising the dead. This pattern was not new to the disciples, for they had witnessed it every day in the ministry of Christ. Indeed, when followers of John the Baptist came to Jesus to inquire about who He was, Christ summarized His own ministry with these words: "Go back and report to John what you hear and see: The blind receive sight, the lame walk, those who have leprosy are cured, the deaf hear, the dead are raised, and the good news is preached to the poor" (Matthew 11:4–5).

The Glory of Salvation Power

Every believer has firsthand experience with God's salvation power. It is the supernatural act by which God delivers us from sin and death and gives us His life through our faith in Jesus Christ, and we are born again. He takes us from darkness and brings us into light, and we begin to see ourselves and the world around us in a new way.

For some, this transformation is nothing short of miraculous as they are delivered from difficulties, such as addictions, and begin a new life of purpose. Their dramatic change is visible to all around them. For too many believers, however, their encounter with the glory of God's power stops there. Many are unaware that the word "salvation" in Greek, *soteria*, means not only salvation but also healing and deliverance as well. Christ's death and resurrection gave us healing and deliverance from oppression, along with our salvation. It is all included in the gift of salvation, freely given to us by God's grace.

The greatest display of this resurrection power was when Jesus Christ was crucified and brought back to life by the power of God through His Spirit. Paul refers to this in his prayer for the church in Ephesus:

> I keep asking that the God of our Lord Jesus Christ, the glorious Father, may give you the Spirit of wisdom and revelation, so that you may know him better. I pray also that the eyes of your heart may be enlightened in order that you may know the hope to which he has called you, the riches of his glorious inheritance in the saints, *and his incomparably great power for us who believe.* That power is like the working of his mighty strength, which he exerted in Christ when he raised him from the dead and seated him at his right hand in the heavenly realms.
>
> Ephesians 1:17–20, emphasis mine

Let's break down this prayer, so we can see all that Paul prays for us:

- He declares the "incomparably great power" that raised Jesus from the dead is available to every believer.
- He prays that we would receive the revelation that this great power is available to us.
- He asks that we would be given wisdom to understand the hope we are called to and how rich our inheritance is.

God wants us to know and actively possess *all*, not just part, of what we have been given in Christ. And part of what we have been given is the heavenly power that dwells within us the moment we accept Jesus Christ as Lord and Savior. However, according to Paul, it takes the Spirit of wisdom and revelation to develop the awareness necessary to implement this power in our everyday experience.

God never commands us to do the impossible. When Jesus commanded us to heal the sick and raise the dead, He was telling us to draw on His own resurrection power, which dwells within us.

Conquering Our Sickness

The resurrection of our Lord gave us eternal life, for which we thank God. If we believe in Him, we will live forever.

For many believers who live with affliction or sickness, healing in heaven is their only hope for the future. They think, "I'll just hang in here with my illness until the rapture comes, or until I die." Their mentality in the meantime is, "I'm suffering for Jesus," or, "I'm taking up my cross."

I do believe that as disciples of Christ we will encounter suffering, but the suffering I see in the New Testament comes from persecution. It is not suffering the way some believers have defined it, where sickness is viewed as a thorn in the flesh or a cross to bear. They believe the trial of suffering with sickness is given to them to help perfect their character. I do not know any parent who would give his or her children any form of sickness to help them grow in character. Yet that is precisely what we project onto our heavenly Father. The truth is, God can help us grow in character without giving us diseases. Yes, God wants us to be holy, but there are other ways He chooses to make us holy.

In his letter to young Timothy, Paul clearly indicates God's method of holy character development. "All Scripture is inspired by God and is useful to teach us what is true and to make us realize what is wrong in our lives. It corrects us when we are wrong and teaches us to do what is right. God uses it to prepare and equip his people to do every good work" (2 Timothy 3:16–17, NLT).

Scripture says Jesus conquered not only our sin on the cross but also our sickness. Paul explains in Romans 8:11, "If the Spirit of him who raised Jesus from the dead is living in you, he who raised Christ from the dead will also give life to your mortal bodies through his Spirit, who lives in you."

For centuries, many in the Church have interpreted this verse to mean: "When you die, God will raise your body, and you'll go to heaven." But the verse actually says the Spirit dwelling within us will give life to our *mortal* bodies. And that means it will happen now, in this earthly life, because now is the only time we have a mortal body. Our mortal bodies won't need life in heaven, because we won't have our mortal bodies there! According to Paul, the same Spirit that raised Jesus from the dead dwells within every believer and can quicken our mortal bodies, healing any disease.

Please do not misunderstand: I encourage all believers to contend and wage war against sickness, in every way possible. There is no condemnation in fighting sickness or in going to a doctor. I believe in doctors. Yet I also believe we are to contend for supernatural, miraculous healings from God, not only for ourselves, but also for others. We are to live supernatural lives, demonstrating the glory of God's power. According to Jesus and the apostle Paul, that is the norm for biblical Christianity.

Healing in Our Midst

As we grow in our relationship with the Lord, we become more aware of how to receive impartations of His glory and power. We walk in greater authority in the Spirit, and signs and wonders—including healing—are demonstrated in our lives.

We are seeing this happen at Harvest Rock Church. We believe and teach that healing is our inheritance now, and we expect healings to occur. And they do! Increasingly, healings are occurring outside of our church services. Let me share with you a few recent examples.

Cancer Healed

Richard and Andrea, a couple in our church, opened their home to host a small group meeting on a night in January 2008, when the group's regular leaders were out of town. At the time, Andrea's mother, Bertilla, was staying in their home. Bertilla had been diagnosed with both breast and lung cancer and was receiving treatment from City of Hope Hospital. That night during the small group meeting, the members anointed Bertilla with oil, laid hands on her and prayed for her. Immediately, she felt better.

The following week, Bertilla went to her appointment with doctors at City of Hope. The cancer tumor in her breast had been the size of an apple. But as the doctors examined her during this appointment, they found no sign of cancer in her body. They decided to conduct a thorough examination and were amazed to discover that the lump had disappeared. Their only explanation was, "Sometimes these things happen."

God completely healed Bertilla of both breast and lung cancer. And I want to emphasize that her healing came not because either I, a pastor, or even the group leaders had prayed for her, but after lay believers in our church prayed for her. God's glory came through His people, plain and simple, releasing the resurrection power that completely healed Bertilla of cancer.

Life Birthed

Another member of our church, Hannah, also received a touch of God's glory through His healing, restorative power.

At the close of our April conference in 2007, my wife, Sue, received a word of knowledge from the Lord that He wanted to release His power through the children in our church. Throughout the conference she sensed that God wanted to release His glory through the children. Now Sue was moved to declare, "If any of our teachers have health problems, please, come forward. We want the children to pray for you."

Hannah, who was helping with the first graders that day, went forward to receive prayer. She and her husband, Sam, wanted to have children. Hannah had already endured two miscarriages and two D-and-C procedures, which the doctors had botched. As a result of the surgeries, she had lived for months with a sharp pain in her abdomen.

As the children prayed for Hannah, she felt the power of God moving within her. She was instantly healed of her pain, and to this day that pain has never returned. Soon afterward, Hannah became pregnant. And today she and Sam are the parents of a beautiful, healthy baby son, Joel.

A Medical Miracle

As we continue to pray for healing of the sick at Harvest Rock Church, God gives us greater miracles. I am especially excited whenever He heals the incurable and His miraculous work is confirmed with medical proof.

Two years ago, a church member, Monica, was diagnosed with multiple sclerosis, following an initial bout with the disorder that had left her partially paralyzed. Monica had great difficulty walking. An MRI conducted at the time indicated the presence of white plaques in her brain, which are characteristic of the disease.

Monica began to pray and believe for her healing, and our prayer teams regularly prayed for her. This continued for eighteen months with no sign of improvement in her condition. But recently, after receiving prayer, Monica's symptoms completely disappeared.

Monica knew she had been divinely healed. She consulted her doctor, who saw that she had dramatically returned to normal physical functioning. He wanted to repeat the MRI procedure, however, to confirm this. The exam revealed that the white plaques had disappeared, showing Monica to be completely normal. Her doctor told her he had no medical explanation for the change in her MRI.

The Glory of Resurrection Power

Many Christians believe that God heals people, because stories of medically unexplainable healings are common. But many of us have great difficulty believing God still raises the dead. We are aware that Jesus raised people from the dead, but we generally consider those incidences to be isolated and relegated to His ministry while on earth. Yet I'm convinced we wouldn't feel this way if we understood *why* Jesus raised the dead.

In John 11, we read of Mary and Martha sending word to Jesus that their brother, Lazarus, was gravely ill. Jesus' response to this news was unusual: "This sickness is not to end in death, but for the glory of God" (John 11:4, NASB). He was signaling to the sisters that Lazarus' illness, though it looked fatal, would result in a display of glory to the Lord.

By the time Jesus arrived on the scene, Lazarus had already been dead for four days and sealed in a tomb. But when Jesus prayed to the Father and called out, "Lazarus, come out!" his friend came back to life, still wrapped in grave clothes (see John 11:41–44).

This is one of the greatest miracles recorded in the New Testament. And Jesus was very clear about the purpose of this miracle: "This sickness is not to end in death, but for the glory of God." Christ raised Lazarus from the dead for the purpose of revealing the glory of God. Later in the same chapter, he states, "Did I not tell you that if you believed, you would see the *glory of God?*" (John 11:40, emphasis mine).

The resurrection of Lazarus foreshadowed the "exceeding great power" that God would soon release in raising Christ from the dead, and through Christ, would impart to us. Lazarus' resurrection was a sign of God's glory revealed as His power. Now I have a question for you. If the people who lived in Christ's time, who could "see" the resurrected Christ, were given Lazarus brought back to life as a sign, do you think that, as God wills, He might provide similar signs today? I can assure you that He does, and in ever increasing numbers.

Dead Raised

From all around the world, I receive reports of God's resurrection power bringing the dead back to life. Rolland and Heidi Baker, Founders of Iris Ministries, have seen more than eighty people raised from the dead in their ministry in Africa, Europe and Asia. Pastor Supresa Sithole partners with the Bakers, serving as International Director of Pastors for Iris Ministries. Supresa had an amazing experience the first time God used him to raise someone from the dead.

In February 2001, Supresa was conducting a crusade in the community hall of Komatipoort, a small town on the border of Mozambique. One day the area chief informed Supresa he would need to suspend the meetings because a six-year-old girl had died the night before. The village wanted to quietly mourn her death.

Supresa asked if he could see the child, and the chief agreed. When he arrived, the girl was still in her bed, cold and stiff. Supresa felt led to pray for her healing. So he began praying for her at midmorning, as the girl's mother and six other women sat with him in the room. As the hours passed and Supresa continued in prayer, the women tired and eventually left the room. Filled with compassion, yet not knowing what to do, Supresa just kept praying, his fingers resting on the mat beside the dead girl.

Sometime that afternoon, as Supresa was in mid-prayer, he felt something touch his hand. He looked up to see that the little girl had grabbed his finger. She was sitting up as if she had just awakened from a deep sleep. She had come back to life!

Supresa ran to tell the mother and the other women, who were shocked to see the little girl sitting up, alive. They began weeping, laughing and dancing. For the next two weeks, many in the village came to believe in Jesus and were saved, after this glorious demonstration of God's resurrection power.

Perhaps one of the most well-known, modern-day resurrections is that of Nigerian pastor Daniel Ekechukwu, which was documented on video by international evangelist Reinhard Bonnke. Daniel died after being involved in a car crash when his brakes failed. He was taken to a hospital where he was pronounced dead on arrival and a death certificate was issued. His body was in a morgue for two days, and the mortician had already injected his body with a chemical solution in preparation for embalming.

Even though rigor mortis had set in, Daniel's wife, prompted by the Holy Spirit, believed she was going to receive him back from the dead. She had his body, already in a coffin, placed in an ambulance and taken to a Reinhard Bonnke conference being held in a neighboring Nigerian city. Daniel was revived there, resurrected as a group of people prayed over him in the basement of the church where the conference was being held. Daniel's resurrection was not only filmed, but eyewitness accounts of numerous witnesses—including those who prayed over his body, the doctor who issued the death certificate and the mortician who was preparing his body for burial— were also documented. This and a number of other healing miracles, resurrections and creative signs and wonders are thoroughly researched and documented by Jane Rumph in her book, *Signs and Wonders in America Today*.[1]

These mighty miracles demonstrate that the same Spirit who raised Jesus from the dead lives within every believer. We all have the potential to see God's glory released through us with evidence of His mighty resurrection power.

A Supernatural Lifestyle

Jesus knew that we were to proclaim the Good News to the world with the glory of God's power following and being manifested in signs and wonders. In fact, He commanded us to spread the Gospel in this way. The impossible becomes possible for us because of the power that lives within us. Romans 6:4 says, "We were therefore buried with him through baptism into death in order that, just as Christ was raised from the dead through the glory of the Father, we too may live a new life." Christ's death and resurrection give every believer access to new life, both in eternity and here on earth.

Jesus told us that the new life He would give us was an abundant life (see John 10:10). Abundant life is life overflowing. It is life filled with such power that it transforms us and the world around us. Abundant life is a supernatural lifestyle. My prayer is that every believer receives the Spirit of wisdom and revelation to understand that we each have access to His glory, to His resurrection power and to His supernatural abundant life here on earth.

5

The Glory of God for Intimacy

God gives us His glory so we may be one with Him. His desire
for us is to share oneness with Him just as Jesus did. This
oneness is foundational, if we are to possess the supernatural
abundant life He desires to give us. Out of this intimacy with
Him, God pours His glory through our lives in several ways.
First, our intimacy with Him empowers us to love others,
enabling us to walk in unity with other believers. Second,
our intimacy with God is the key to evangelism and societal
transformation in the world around us.

We see these things detailed in Jesus' prayer to the Father
in John's gospel:

> "My prayer is not for them alone. I pray also for those who
> will believe in me through their message, that all of them
> may be one, Father, just as you are in me and I am in you.
> May they also be in us so that the world may believe that
> you have sent me. *I have given them the glory that you gave
> me, that they may be one as we are one: I in them and you
> in me*. May they be brought to complete unity to let the

world know that you sent me and have loved them even as you have loved me.

John 17:20–23, emphasis mine

Traditionally, this prayer has been interpreted as Jesus' desire for all believers to be in unity with each other, just as Jesus is in unity with the Father. But I believe that if we examine the text carefully, we can see there is a more important oneness that Jesus is referring to. Yes, God desires us to be in unity as the Body of Christ, but more significantly God has given us His glory so that we can be one with Him.

We know that Jesus has perfect unity with the Father. In John 17, when Jesus prayed that all those who believed in the disciples' message would be one, He was referring to every believer who would ever come to know Him, including you and me. And His prayer is that we all would become one with the Father, just as He is one with the Father.

This unique "oneness" is best reflected in the life of Christ. John tells us that Jesus Christ existed with God in the beginning because He was God (see John 1:1). Even before Abraham lived, Jesus existed (see John 8:58). It is important to remember that when Jesus came to earth, He chose to set aside His divinity. This means that He did nothing as God, but accomplished everything living as a man in complete unity with the Father and the Holy Spirit. Even as the Son of God who took on flesh, Jesus was still completely dependent on His Father during His time here on earth. Jesus did only what He saw the Father do (see John 5:19), and He was continually moved with compassion and performed amazing miracles. Through His life on earth, Jesus demonstrated what a life of oneness with the Father looks like. And according to Jesus, we now have access to that same life of oneness with the Father, and are to reflect His goodness and power to the world around us.

Jesus says He has given us His glory for the purpose of oneness: "*I have given them the glory that you gave me, that they may be one as we are one."* When we receive Jesus Christ, we are given access to His glory, which enables us to live in oneness with the Father, His Son and the Holy Spirit.

Our Unity with the Father, the Son, and the Holy Spirit

I share the desire of the apostle Paul, who prayed this near the end of his life: "I want to know Christ and the power of his resurrection and the fellowship of sharing in his sufferings, becoming like him in his death" (Philippians 3:10). When Paul prayed this, he had already experienced God in a number of significant ways. He had a vision of Jesus on the road to Damascus (see Acts 9:4–9). And he was caught up to "the third heaven" in a powerful vision (see 2 Corinthians 12:2). Yet after all these things, Paul wanted to know Christ more deeply.

This oneness with God that we receive as a result of our relationship with Christ is expressed in both *positional intimacy* and *progressive intimacy.* Our *positional* intimacy— meaning, our access to God—is what we are given at the point of our salvation. By receiving Jesus we immediately become a child of God, and through that relationship, we are given open access to the Father.

But our God is infinite and eternal, and there is always more to know and experience of Him. This is what is known as *progressive* intimacy. Jesus has given us His glory toward this purpose. Paul states it this way: "I consider everything a loss compared to the surpassing greatness of knowing Christ Jesus my Lord, for whose sake I have lost all things. I consider them rubbish, that I may gain Christ" (Philippians 3:8).

We have been given a great privilege and a costly gift. Through Jesus' death and resurrection, and the presence of His Holy Spirit in us, we are able to walk in unity daily with the Creator of the universe. God has done all to reconcile us to Himself, to the point of sending His own Son as a sacrifice for our sins. He has opened His arms wide to us, desiring intimacy with us. It is up to us to respond by actively pursuing an intimate relationship with Him. Intimacy with the Father is limitless!

Our Unity with Each Other

When we walk in unity with God, unity with other believers becomes a beautiful by-product. As John states in his first epistle, "We love because he first loved us" (1 John 4:19). When we are filled daily with God's love through the Holy Spirit, we are filled with the fruits of His Spirit: love, joy, peace, patience, kindness, goodness, faithfulness, gentleness and self-control (see Galatians 5:22–23). Our intimacy with Him causes us to overflow with God's glory, and we will radiate His love.

The way to have such love for each other is found in intimacy with Jesus. Jesus says, "I am the vine; you are the branches. If a man remains in me and I in him, he will bear much fruit; apart from me you can do nothing" (John 15:5). As we abide in Christ He abides in us, and we will bear much fruit.

He also gives us His glory to empower us to have unity with other believers. Just a few verses later, He gives us this command: "My command is this: Love each other as I have loved you" (John 15:12). Apart from Jesus, it is impossible to fulfill this command. But if we abide in Him and He abides in us, we will bear much fruit in oneness with other believers. He will give us the glory to come into unity. And when we receive love from God, we will be able to love others as He loves us.

This twofold unity—with the triune God and with each other—is the key to evangelism. Indeed, our intimacy with God has everything to do with His great harvest. Jesus said, "May they be brought to complete unity *to let the world know* that you sent me and have loved them even as you have loved me" (John 17:23, emphasis mine). It is through our oneness with God and His people that His glory is revealed through us, leading the world to believe in Him.

Intimacy Manifested as Goodness

Out of our intimacy with God, His glory will be manifested through us both in *goodness* and in *power*.

God's *goodness* is made evident in our love for Him and for each other. When I was a student at the University of Maryland, a young woman I didn't know asked me, "Why are you always smiling?" I was surprised at this, as I didn't know I had been smiling. Her question made me realize I was filled with joy because of my relationship with the Lord. This opened the door for me to share the Gospel with her, and she gave her heart to Jesus.

Winkie Pratney, the well-known youth minister and evangelist, has said that the two most effective ways to evangelize are to bring unbelievers into a Christian community where people love each other, and to bring the Christian community into the world and let unbelievers see that we love each other. Both ways, the world will be won to Jesus Christ through our love.

A Demonstration of Love

Several years ago, in one of the Marxist nations of Africa, a missionary was arrested for refusing to leave the country. He was imprisoned in a cell he shared with a mass murderer. The missionary attempted to share the Gospel with the murderer, but the murderer had no intention of receiving Jesus. The missionary then decided he would demonstrate Christ's love in a practical way by giving the murderer a part of his ration of food. He did this every day for several months, until the murderer began to see these were acts of genuine love from the missionary.

One day as they talked, the Lord gave the missionary a word of wisdom. The missionary asked the murderer, "Do you know who Jesus is like?"

The murderer responded, "No, I don't know who Jesus is like."

The missionary told him, "Jesus is like me."

Suddenly, the scales fell from the murderer's eyes. He stated, "If Jesus is like you, then I want to become a follower of Jesus." He gave his life to the Lord.

Many of us say, "I want to be like Jesus." But how many of us can say, "Jesus is like me"? God wants us to be so united in intimacy with Him that we can confidently say, "I am here to represent Jesus."

Christ Himself tells us we are to be carriers of God's glory: "Let your light shine before men, that they may see your good deeds and praise your Father in heaven" (Matthew 5:16). When we have an intimate relationship with God, His glory will shine forth from our lives and demonstrate His goodness to the world through our love, kindness and faithfulness. People can tell whether or not we genuinely love them. When people see the glory of God demonstrated through our love for them, they will be able to recognize His goodness and come to know Him.

Intimacy Manifested as Power

Through our intimacy with God, His glory is released in us as *power to reach the lost*. God's power can heal the sick, cast out demons and raise the dead. And we are called to bring this power of God wherever we go (see Matthew 10:8).

Church leaders have commonly believed we would see revival and harvest if we hosted more prayer gatherings, with pastors, especially, praying together and doing more to bring unity to the Body of Christ. Of course, there is truth to this; we do need prayer and unity in the Body of Christ. But throughout history, there have been many prayer meetings, prayer summits and unity meetings that have not brought about a harvest.

The Bible tells us "the kingdom of God is not a matter of talk but of power" (1 Corinthians 4:20). Therefore, we usher in the Kingdom of God when we move in His power. And the only way to receive God's power is to receive more of His glory through intimacy with Him. Personal intimacy requires time spent in relationship. When we spend time with God, He will fill us with His power through the Holy Spirit, and we will be able to preach the Gospel, moving in signs, wonders and miracles.

Herman Martir, a pastor in Dallas with Harvest International Ministry (HIM), told me an encouraging story on this subject that took place in the Philippines. When he was invited to one of the HIM churches there, the Spirit imparted an anointing for healing that was so powerful that the church's members began to move in signs and wonders. They decided to go to the local hospitals to pray for the sick to be healed. Herman said so many miraculous healings occurred in those hospitals that fifteen doctors were saved. Those physicians were thoroughly trained in scientific thinking, yet God's display of His glory to miraculously heal was so manifestly powerful that they were drawn to Jesus.

God's people are taking His power into society, and people are being saved. When we are connected to God in intimacy, we will flow in the supernatural and as a result we can see a great harvest of souls for His Kingdom.

Developing Unity with God

What keeps you from having the oneness with God that Jesus had with the Father? God has already given us His glory so that we may be one with Him (see John 17:22). And Jesus says the Father desires to give us the Kingdom (see Luke 12:32). So, why do we not see more of His glory? Why do we seem to bring about so little of His Kingdom?

I believe the problem is on our side. Salvation through Christ is just the beginning of life in the Kingdom of God. We have been commanded to actively pursue the Lord and His presence. As we spend time in His presence, we receive more of His glory, and we become more like Him.

Yet sometimes, despite our good intentions, we find ourselves repeatedly hindered in pursuing intimacy with God. Whatever keeps you from increased intimacy with Jesus, the Lord will reveal it to you as you seek Him. God's glory and grace have the power to break all hindrances, all bondages of sin or fear, and to set us free (see Psalm 146:7). God has also provided strength and encouragement to us through the members of His Body. If you are struggling with repetitive issues that disrupt your intimacy with God, seek help through trusted friends in the Lord. You may need counseling or prayer for inner healing. Whatever your situation, the journey is always easier when it is shared with others who can help to bear your burden.

Most of all, never think you are the only one who struggles! None of us is perfect, and we all face struggles. James encourages us, "Confess your sins to each other and pray for each other so that you may be healed. The earnest prayer of a righteous person has great power and produces wonderful results" (James 5:16, NLT).

The only way to develop intimacy is to set apart time to be with the Lord and to hunger and thirst for His presence. Without such intimacy with Him, we may know a great deal about God, but we will miss out on knowing Him in a personal way. Of course, there is no formula for achieving intimacy. Just as no two human relationships are identical, so each of us has a unique relationship with the Lord. Intimacy will occur as we seek His presence in the ways that are most meaningful to us. For some this means spending time in prayer, while others may find that meditating on Scripture is most helpful. Still others soak up God's presence by listening to worship music, while others find Him in complete silence.

I want to be a friend of God. And I want to be intimate with Him daily. The Bible says God reveals things to His friends and entrusts them with His authority and power. Therefore, let us pursue a life of oneness with the Lord. As we do, He will shine His glory through us. And we will see released in us both His goodness and His power, impacting others for the glory of His Kingdom.

6

Destined for Glory

So far in this book, we have discussed the glory of God as His manifest presence, released in the form of His goodness and His power. Yet just as a diamond has many facets, the glory of God has many more dimensions than this. In this chapter, I want to talk about another type of glory God has given us. This glory comes in the form of *honor* and is an important aspect of the supernatural, abundant life God gives to us.

Crowned with Glory and Honor

According to the psalmist, from the very beginning of creation, God crowned man with glory, honor and majesty (see Psalm 8:5). Amazed at this truth, David sings:

> When I consider Your heavens, the work of Your fingers, the moon and the stars, which You have ordained; what is man that You take thought of him, and the son of man that

You care for him? Yet You have made him a little lower than God, and You crown him with glory and majesty! You make him to rule over the works of Your hands; You have put all things under his feet, all sheep and oxen, and also the beasts of the field, the birds of the heavens, and the fish of the sea, whatever passes through the paths of the seas.

Psalm 8:3–8, NASB

Originally humanity was created in God's image, to glorify God by having a derived glory that comes from obedience to God, communion with God and being filled with God's Spirit. Unfortunately humanity chose a different path, and we lost our original purpose and destiny. But God never deviated from His original intent. He created humanity for glory, and He will not allow us to permanently settle for less. Sometimes we Christians become so focused on our sins and Christ's redemption we overlook the reality that God wants to do more than just erase our "sin slate." He intends to restore us to the original state of glory, honor and dominion for which He created us. Our story as humanity is a familiar three-part play, and I want to briefly review it with God's purpose and destiny for us in view.

When God created Adam and Eve, He gave them glory and honor by creating them in His own image. He made humankind a little lower than Himself. Genesis tells us that God blessed Adam and Eve and told them to "be fruitful and increase in number; fill the earth and subdue it" (Genesis 1:28). God created humankind to rule with Him over all of creation, to take dominion over the earth.

But the glory that was given to man from God was lost through sin. Humankind lost much of the glory that God intended for us by rebelling against the Lord, making alternative choices we thought were better and falling into sin (see Genesis 3). Paul alludes to the Fall and its effects in Romans 3:23: "All have sinned and fall short of the glory of God."

Thankfully, God reclaimed the glory of humankind through the finished work of Jesus Christ, who died for our sin, rose again, ascended into heaven and is now seated at the right hand of the Father (see Hebrews 12:2). Jesus died to restore the glory that God destined to be ours from the beginning. Paul tells us: "We speak of God's secret wisdom, a wisdom that has been hidden and that God destined for our glory before time began. None of the rulers of this age understood it, for if they had, they would not have crucified the Lord of glory" (1 Corinthians 2:7–8).

Paul clearly indicates that by crucifying Jesus Christ, Satan unknowingly cooperated with God's plan, restoring humankind into the glory that God intended for us since before time began. If Satan had known the true extent of what he was doing by crucifying Jesus, he never would have made that mistake. But now, the Bible says, "God raised us up with Christ and seated us with him in the heavenly realms in Christ Jesus" (Ephesians 2:6). Through Jesus, the glory of humankind has been restored, and we can now properly participate in the glory that God originally intended for us.

What an amazing truth! Yet even as we accept this—that God crowns us with glory, honor and majesty—we are not to take the glory of God upon ourselves. In other words, we are not to receive man's praises for glory that rightfully belongs to God. The Lord will not share His glory with anyone (see Isaiah 42:8). But as His children we are destined to reflect God's glory as He bestows it on us. In this way, we glorify God with the very glory He has given us.

This glory is all part of our inheritance and destiny in Christ. And we must learn how to walk in this incredible glory that God has given us. Yet many believers struggle to do this. Unfortunately, many of us live like paupers instead of the royalty God has made us to be. Instead of walking in His confidence, believing we can do all things through Christ (see Philippians 4:13), we lack self-esteem, feeling utterly inadequate to face the challenges of life.

I want to share with you five practical steps for walking in the glory that God has restored to us. I have learned these steps through my own life experiences and struggles.

1. Know Your Identity in Christ

To walk in the glory God has intended for us, it is crucial we renew our minds to properly understand who we are in Christ. The Bible tells us, "As (a man) thinks within himself, so he is" (Proverbs 23:7, NASB). Whatever we believe about ourselves deep within our hearts, we will become. The inner life manifests in the outward man.

The difficulty in understanding our true identity in Christ stems from the fact we have a deceitful and malicious enemy, Satan. The devil constantly accuses us, filling our minds with thoughts of how worthless we are, pointing out all our flaws and failures, making us feel shame, guilt and despair. Before we knew the Lord, most of us lived with and believed this accuser of the brethren (as Jesus called him). Today, much of our thought life, patterns of behavior and lifestyle reflect those years of oppression before we knew Christ. When we are saved, our spirits are renewed by God's Spirit, but we are still subject to our old minds and bodies. This is why Paul tells us, "Do not be conformed to this world, but be transformed by the renewing of your mind" (Romans 12:2, NASB). We are able to constantly renew our minds by immersing ourselves in God's Word. If we meditate on the Bible day and night, and live according to all that is written in it, we are promised our lives will be prosperous and successful (see Joshua 1:7–8).

I can testify to this truth, because the Bible has transformed my mind. My thinking has completely changed since I learned from the Spirit how to meditate on God's Word. And the most important thing I have learned is who I am in Christ.

Do you know what the Bible says about you? Scripture tells us these things about our identity in Him:

- God calls us His children: "How great is the love the Father has lavished on us, that we should be called children of God! And that is what we are!" (1 John 3:1).
- God calls us joint heirs with Jesus: "The Spirit himself testifies with our spirit that we are God's children. Now if we are children, then we are heirs—heirs of God and co-heirs with Christ, if indeed we share in his sufferings in order that we may also share in his glory" (Romans 8:16–17).
- God calls us His ambassadors: "We are ambassadors for Christ" (2 Corinthians 5:20, NASB).
- God calls us kings and priests: "And has made us kings and priests to His God and Father, to Him be glory and dominion forever and ever" (Revelation 1:6, NKJV).
- God calls us righteous: "He made Him who knew no sin to be sin on our behalf, so that we might become the righteousness of God in Him" (2 Corinthians 5:21, NASB).

By learning to see ourselves as God sees us, we begin to know who we are in Christ. Then we are able to walk properly in the glory, honor and majesty He has crowned us with.

2. Humble Yourself and God Will Exalt You

God has destined us for glory, but He will not honor us if we harbor selfish ambition or pride. God knows our heart (see 1 Samuel 16:7). And His Word commands, "Humble yourselves in the presence of the Lord, and He will exalt you" (James 4:10, NASB).

Humility is a choice. God says that when we commit to give Him all the praise and glory we receive, He will exalt us. But when we strive and act driven by selfish ambition, this is earthly, natural and even demonic (see James 3:15). It is good and honoring to God if we want to be used by Him, seeking to fulfill our destiny and calling in Christ. But if we operate out of improper and impure motives, we are exercising unsanctified zeal.

In the world, self-promotion and striving are frequent. Of course this also occurs in the church, but a more significant issue among Christians, in my opinion, is false humility and low self-esteem. I see believers constantly downplaying their identities in Christ. In their desire to be humble, they keep looking back at their old identity: "I'm just a sinner saved by grace." They don't grasp their new identity in Christ. In this way, they fail to walk in the glory God has given them.

God's desire is to give us the Kingdom and every blessing that goes with it (see Luke 12:32). God isn't holding anything back from us. He has provided all we need to prosper, to be promoted, to be the head and not the tail (see Deuteronomy 28:13). He wants us to receive His glory so that we may be transformed into the image of Jesus and reflect His glory into the world. He has destined us to walk in sonship and royalty, as kings and priests. True humility is joyfully receiving all God gives to us and acknowledging who He has made us to be in Christ.

We know that when we humble ourselves in this way, God will exalt us (see James 4:10). And when God chooses to exalt us, we must learn to receive and walk in the glory and honor He bestows on us.

3. Do Everything with Excellence

God wants us to excel in both inward character and outward actions. "Just as you excel in everything—in faith, in speech, in knowledge, in complete earnestness and in your love for us—see that you also excel in this grace of giving"

(2 Corinthians 8:7). "Whatever your hand finds to do, do it with all your might" (Ecclesiastes 9:10).

The pursuit of excellence is both the goal and the mark of spiritual maturity, as long as it is motivated by the right values, priorities and motives. With the gifts and abilities God has given us, we are to do our best for His glory. And as we actively pursue excellence, inward or outward, God can trust us with more of His glory. As this glory transforms our character on the inside, it will also manifest as favor and promotion on the outside.

Everything that God has done He has done with excellence. When God created the heavens and the earth, He saw all that He had made and deemed it to be very good (see Genesis 1:31). "Praise the LORD in song, for He has done excellent things; let this be known throughout the earth" (Isaiah 12:5, NASB). Likewise, God calls His people to reflect this aspect of excellence in His nature.

Yet the Lord not only calls us to excellence, He also provides us with the tools to overcome the obstacles that prevent us from it. Peter writes, "His divine power has granted to us everything pertaining to life and godliness, through the true knowledge of Him who called us by His own glory and excellence" (2 Peter 1:3, NASB). Because God has called us by His own glory and excellence, there should be no ceiling for us whatsoever.

Consider the powerful testimony of Bishop Tudor Bismark, pastor of one of the largest churches in Africa, located in Zimbabwe. I had the privilege of meeting Bishop Tudor at a conference in Dallas. Zimbabwe's president, Robert Mugabe, had stolen the national election, and the country was suffering under hyperinflation and human rights abuses. The unemployment rate was 80 percent. Voices rose from all over the world to cry out for the United Nations to intervene.

Meanwhile, in the midst of these dark circumstances, Bishop Tudor was pastoring a mega-church of over ten thousand people. Incredibly, 80 percent of people in his church held jobs—an amazing statistic in a nation with such massive unemployment. Bishop Tudor built into his church's DNA the expectation of the impossible. If anyone would get jobs, it would be God's people. He taught them that Jesus is bigger than any demonic force, including those forces that influence economics, unemployment or politics.

We are not to limit the Holy One of Israel in our lives. Each of us has an individual and unique destiny, according to God's design. Simply put, we can be whatever God calls us to be. And we can be excellent in all of our actions and moral character, because God has given us His grace in everything pertaining to life and godliness. Therefore, we can declare with Paul, "I press on to take hold of that for which Christ Jesus took hold of me" (Philippians 3:12).

4. Learn How to Honor Others

Before God can exalt us, we must learn to submit in humility. Scripture says the Lord gives grace to the humble (see Proverbs 3:34). If we are to receive honor, we must first learn how to give honor to others. Honoring others causes the favor of God to flow into our lives.

Our honor and favor come *from* God, yet they arrive *through* people. For example, promotions come as a direct result of receiving favor from earthly bosses. And our supervisors are more inclined to promote us if they feel honored and respected by us. Little gestures, like giving your manager a birthday card, can effectively communicate honor. Some people cannot find it in their hearts to honor their bosses, for whatever reason. Yet they still must learn how to properly respect and bless authority as a part of God's order. In this way, His blessings will flow into their lives.

Consider the Fourth Commandment: It tells us that if we honor our parents, our lives will be blessed. "Honor your father and your mother, as the LORD your God has commanded you, so that you may live long and that it may go well with you in the land the LORD your God is giving you" (Deuteronomy 5:16). It doesn't matter whether our parents are Christians or even honorable. We are told that if we honor them, as a part of God's order, things will go well with us. God releases His favor and blessing into our lives whenever we honor those He has placed in authority over us.

I can testify that God's blessings have been released into my life as I have properly aligned myself under both spiritual and earthly authority. If we understand how to honor others and how to properly align ourselves under God-given authority, the honor and favor of the Lord will be released abundantly in our lives. This is critical for staying in the flow of God's glory, a subject we'll look at in greater detail in a later chapter.

5. Learn to Ask God and Others for Favor

God has destined us for glory. Yet many in the Body of Christ have not received the glory, honor and majesty God intends for them. Why is this so? James gives us one answer to this question: "You do not have, because you do not ask God. When you ask, you do not receive, because you ask with wrong motives, that you may spend what you get on your pleasures" (James 4:2–3).

God is the One who opens and closes doors. He is the giver of every good and perfect gift (see James 1:17). We simply need to learn to ask the Lord for our heart's desires. Jesus tells us, "Ask and it will be given to you; seek and you will find; knock and the door will be opened to you" (Matthew 7:7). When we ask God for something, according to His will, it will be given to us.

Yet when we ask, our motives must be pure. According to James, when we do not receive what we have asked for, we may have asked with improper motives (see James 4:3). I constantly ask God to search my heart, to show me if I am pure in my intentions and ambitions—particularly when I ask for favor or for doors to open.

Many times, the proper way to ask for favor includes a genuine willingness to die to our desires. In answer to our requests, God may say, "Yes," "No," or "Not yet." But no matter what His response, the Bible tells us, "Trust in the LORD with all your heart and lean not on your own understanding; in all your ways acknowledge him, and he will make your paths straight" (Proverbs 3:5–6). We must be willing to trust in God's goodness and faithfulness, even if our requests are denied, because God knows what is best for our lives.

The Lord desires to give good gifts to His children, and we should expect to see His blessings through earthly means such as promotions, checks in the mail, restored relationships and more. Jesus tells us, "If you, then, though you are evil, know how to give good gifts to your children, how much more will your Father in heaven give good gifts to those who ask him!" (Matthew 7:11). If we learn to ask God and others for favor, and we have the correct character, integrity and motives, the Lord will pour out the glory and honor He has destined for us from the very beginning of time.

Walking in Glory

God has done everything in His power to restore His glory to us. Through the sacrificial death and resurrection of Jesus, we now have access to the glory, honor and majesty He ordained for us in our creation. We can rule and reign with Him on the earth, taking dominion over the darkness. He wants us to walk in the glory He has given us, in order to bring more glory to His name.

As we receive God's glory, we will reflect it in the world. And when God's children are seen walking in the glory, honor and promotion He has provided, the world will begin to see God as He truly is. Then they will come to see Jesus as the true Savior of the world.

7

The Glory of God and Personal Holiness

On March 22, 2008, Cindy Jacobs, a close friend and someone I consider a major prophetess in the Body of Christ, gave a prophetic word to our church. One part of this word was as follows: "The Lord is going to release a sweeping holiness movement, so He can open the door to a glory movement such as the earth has not seen."

Cindy didn't know that only a few weeks earlier Peter Wagner, a mentor to me and President of Global Harvest Ministries, had brought up the subject of holiness during an afternoon session with the leaders in our church. Peter is seen by many as a leading apostle in the Body of Christ, and that day he told us, "The strongest message I have is the message of holiness." He gave an example from his life, saying, "I have not sinned all day today, and I don't plan to sin for the rest of the day." He thought for a moment before adding, "In fact, yesterday I didn't sin. I didn't sin the day before. And I don't plan to sin tomorrow."

I was initially stunned when I heard this. Peter shared this with us not as a boast but as a simple fact—a fact that made me introspective. I asked myself, "Have I sinned today, as far as breaking any biblical commandments?" After pondering this, I realized I hadn't sinned that day. Then I realized I hadn't sinned the day before. And I certainly didn't plan to sin the next day.

As I thought about it, I realized that earlier in my life, this would have been a very difficult thing to do. But now it is relatively easy for me. Like Peter, I do not share this to boast. I share it only to point out that Peter's time with us made me realize we *can* progress in our ability to lead a holy life.

This gives me hope and encourages me, for the Lord calls us to holiness. Indeed, He commands us to be holy even as He is holy. This sounds impossible, but I know the Lord never tells us to do something impossible. When He calls us to holiness, He calls us simply to surrender to His grace, which will make us holy.

Consider what God says through the prophet Isaiah:

> The Lord will wash away the filth of the women of Zion; he will cleanse the bloodstains from Jerusalem by a spirit of judgment and a spirit of fire. Then the LORD will create over all of Mount Zion and over those who assemble there a cloud of smoke by day and a glow of flaming fire by night; over all the glory will be a canopy.
>
> Isaiah 4:4–5

We see in this passage that God makes His people holy by His Spirit. It is impossible for us to be holy apart from a work of grace by the power of His Holy Spirit. It is then—after God releases holiness in us—that He sends His glory and that glory covers us like a canopy. Isaiah describes this process of holiness preceding glory:

> "In the desert prepare the way for the LORD; make straight in the wilderness a highway for our God. Every valley shall be raised up, every mountain and hill made low; the rough ground shall become level, the rugged places a plain. And the glory of the LORD will be revealed, and all mankind together will see it."
>
> Isaiah 40:3–5

In Isaiah, we see that a highway of holiness must be prepared before the glory of the Lord will be revealed. God is going to straighten things out before He comes back. He is going to make us holy.

What is Holiness?

Legalism vs. License

It is important for us to pursue holiness. As the author of Hebrews says, "Without holiness no one will see the Lord" (Hebrews 12:14). But to be holy, we must first define what holiness is.

Sadly, much of the Church today does not know what it means to be holy. On one side, a religious spirit has infiltrated the church, filling it with legalism and standards that are not consistent with biblical absolutes. On the other side, there has been an overemphasis on extreme grace, giving followers of Christ tremendous license to sin.

This is not a new problem in the Church. Nearly two thousand years ago, in his letter to the churches in Galatia, Paul dealt with both kinds of groups. On one extreme of the Galatian church body were Messianic Jews, who believed that people could not truly be saved unless they were circumcised.

95

Paul had to tell them their belief was not biblical (see Galatians 2). On the other extreme in the church, some Gentile believers were involved in immorality, envy and drunkenness. Paul had to warn them, "Those who live like this will not inherit the kingdom of God" (Galatians 5:21).

Paul went back and forth in the letter, addressing each group alternately. He understood that they came from different starting points in the faith and that each needed a different kind of correction. The Messianic Jews came to Christ from a background of radical obedience, so Paul emphasized grace to them. The Gentile believers came from a background of licentiousness, so Paul emphasized to them the consequences of works of the flesh. I believe his letter effectively depicts a similar condition afflicting too many in the Church today, with both extremes still in place.

Biblical Definition

The Greek New Testament word for holiness is *hagios*, which means "to be set apart." Once we are born again, the Lord sets us apart for Himself, as His people. God brings us into holiness—a right relationship with Him—through our faith in Jesus. Our position in Christ confers His holiness upon us.

So, on one hand, we are already holy. Peter tells us, "You are a chosen people, a royal priesthood, a holy nation, a people belonging to God, that you may declare the praises of him who called you out of darkness into his wonderful light" (1 Peter 2:9). This is why Paul addressed his letters to the "saints" in the churches in Ephesus, Corinth and others. In fact, all believers are saints. The Bible says, "God made him who had no sin to be sin for us, so that in him we might become the righteousness of God" (2 Corinthians 5:21). The reality of our holiness in Christ can be very difficult for us to accept. As we begin to renew our minds by meditating on

God's Word, we are able to receive it. We understand that once we receive Jesus we have right standing with God.

It is important that we understand we are made holy in Christ. On the other hand, are we holy enough? To be holy also means being *set apart from sin*. Scripture says we are made the righteousness of God in Christ (see 2 Corinthians 5:21), which is a conferred position of holiness. But we can always grow in the holiness of our conduct.

Daily we can choose to consecrate ourselves, setting our lives apart for God and His service. We do this by actively departing from sin and obeying His Word. Moreover, we follow the model of Jesus and align our conduct with God's will. This isn't an instant accomplishment; we progressively learn holiness, pursuing it one step at a time. I think of it this way: I was saved; I am being saved; I will be saved. In short, I *was saved* when I accepted Jesus. Today I am in the process of *being sanctified*. And I *will be saved* at the Second Coming of Jesus. The Lord's desire is for us to grow and mature in our holiness.

Often what we think is holiness is not actually in line with biblical standards. Our ideas of holiness may be *derived* from biblical standards, but they may also be influenced by cultural standards and personal preferences. Problems arise when we elevate our cultural standards or personal preferences to the level of biblical standards.

Biblical Standards

The Bible's standards for holiness are clear. The Ten Commandments give distinct rules in Exodus 20. These are: Do not worship other gods, do not have idols, do not misuse God's name, observe the Sabbath day, honor your father and mother, do not murder, do not commit adultery, do not steal, do not lie and do not covet.

In the New Testament, Paul gives similar guidelines. To the church in Galatia, he writes: "The acts of the sinful nature are obvious: sexual immorality, impurity and debauchery; idolatry and witchcraft; hatred, discord, jealousy, fits of rage, selfish ambition, dissensions, factions and envy; drunkenness, orgies, and the like" (Galatians 5:19).

In writing to the Colossians, Paul instructs:

> Put to death, therefore, whatever belongs to your earthly nature: sexual immorality, impurity, lust, evil desires and greed, which is idolatry. You used to walk in these ways, in the life you once lived. But now you must rid yourselves of all such things as these: anger, rage, malice, slander, and filthy language from your lips. Do not lie to each other, since you have taken off your old self with its practices and have put on the new self, which is being renewed in knowledge in the image of its Creator.
>
> Colossians 3:5–10

Any of the sins listed in either the Old Testament or New Testament are clear violations of the biblical standard of holiness.

Cultural Standards and Personal Preferences

The Trap of Legalism

Cultural standards are powerful influences on groups of people. A group may be defined by national, ethnic, political, religious or other membership. All of us belong to multiple groups with different cultural standards. And often we can't be a member of the group if we don't embrace the standards of its culture. Sometimes those standards can get very warped but seem normal to people within the group. For example, in recent years the news media has covered a polygamy cult in Texas, in which the practice of older men marrying child brides is not openly questioned by the cult members. Their silent acceptance seems to us strange and even unhealthy.

But if we are honest, we must admit that, increasingly, we live in a society whose cultural standards keep shifting and placing incredible pressure on us to either conform or risk being considered "intolerant."

In contrast to cultural standards, personal preferences are internal standards that an individual embraces. These can be helpful to the person, but they can't be demanded of others. Both cultural standards and personal preferences change over time. Biblical standards, however, do not, because they are based on God's character and commands. Without His standards, we have no anchor to secure us, no compass to guide our way.

Unfortunately, Christian groups commonly overemphasize certain cultural standards or personal preferences that are outside of biblical standards. An example of this is the issue of watching television. Certain church groups and cultures say watching television is evil. I remember years ago, a member of our church who gave a large tithe focused intensely on this issue. With great solemnity he told me, "Pastor, I have something very serious to discuss with you. And I believe this is the word of the Lord. You need to tell everyone in Harvest Rock Church to throw away their television sets." He was sincerely convinced that this action was necessary for everyone.

I responded, "There may be some people who need to throw away their television set because they are in bondage to it. But for me to legislate that from the pulpit is legalism. And that comes from a religious spirit." Without realizing it, he had elevated a cultural standard and had come to believe it was a biblical standard.

This kind of legalism has occurred repetitively throughout Church history. People have projected their own cultural standards or personal preferences onto the Body of Christ as biblical standards. Wearing makeup became a sin. Wearing jeans or pants became a sin for women. In some denominations, women could not cut their hair because it was considered a sin. Abstaining from movie going was elevated to a biblical standard and so was abstinence from alcohol. The Bible clearly states that drunkenness is a sin, but drinking wine without getting drunk is not (see Galatians 5:21).

The list of cultural standards and personal preferences goes on, prohibiting dancing, playing cards and wearing jewelry. Unfortunately, even today many groups have identified these types of practices to be sin, but that is not what the Bible says. Dancing is not a sin, but someone can make it his personal preference not to dance. Our personal preferences may be very helpful to us in our pursuit of personal holiness, but we must not turn them into general rules of living for everyone else.

The Trap of Licentiousness

If we do not identify and clearly follow God's standards of holiness, we risk falling into the trap of licentiousness. Sexual immorality is a clear violation of biblical standards, but I have heard many engaged couples try to justify having sex before marriage. They say, "We're going to get married anyway, so it's okay for us." But the Bible states that fornication is sin. The biblical order for sex is very clear: chastity before marriage and fidelity after.

It is easy to compromise with licentiousness. We live in a society where telling "white lies" is acceptable "as long as it doesn't hurt anyone." Cheating on your taxes or cutting corners on a business deal is considered smart as long as you don't get caught. And who hasn't exceeded the speed limit while keeping an eye fixed on the rearview mirror?

Adultery is sin. Homosexuality is sin. And so are these other things we think of as "lesser" evils. We need to be very clear about our standards of holiness: The Bible sets these standards, not you or I. We are only practicing holiness when we are obeying God's standards for our lives. And when we depart from them we get into trouble. "There is a way which seems right to a man, but its end is the way of death" (Proverbs 14:12, NASB).

We Do Not Have to Sin

What does the Bible say about Christians and sin? The apostle John tells us, "Whoever abides in Him does not sin. Whoever sins has neither seen Him nor known Him. . . . Whoever has been born of God does not sin, for His seed remains in him; and he cannot sin, because he has been born of God" (1 John 3:6, 9, NKJV).

John makes it clear that, as followers of Jesus, we do not have to sin. We are no longer under the law, but under grace (see Romans 6:14). And if we live under the grace of God, we will not be in bondage to sin. I was a drug addict before I gave my life to the Lord. When I was born again, I was delivered from drugs. By God's grace and transformative power, I have never returned to drug use even once. I simply have no desire for it. My life experience has taught me the truth of Paul's words in Titus 2:11–12: "The grace of God that brings salvation has appeared to all men. It teaches us to say 'No' to ungodliness and worldly passions, and to live self-controlled, upright and godly lives in this present age."

Jesus is coming for a Bride that is holy, without spot or blemish. I believe the Body of Christ can have a revival of holiness that sweeps our churches and the nations.

Followers of Jesus Do Sin

Now let me say something that seems totally contradictory: *Followers of Jesus do sin.* John writes:

If we claim to be without sin, we deceive ourselves and the truth is not in us. If we confess our sins, he is faithful and just and will forgive us our sins and purify us from all unrighteousness. If we claim we have not sinned, we make him out to be a liar and his word has no place in our lives.

1 John 1:8–10

John contrasts the person who sins continually as not being a true child of God. A natural outflow of being in Christ is that we will not habitually practice sin, but this doesn't mean we won't commit sins. Rather, our life isn't one of habitual sin. Our lives naturally become more Christlike as we grow in Him. In short, true Christians no longer live a lifestyle that is characterized by continual sinning. But that does not mean we cannot or do not ever sin. If we are continually filled with the Spirit and are living in grace, we do not have to sin. But if we do sin, there is also grace. This is why we live in the tension of two truths: Christians are already holy, and no Christian can be holy enough. Only when we get to heaven will we be totally free from the possibility of sin entering our lives.

Walking Out Holiness

Charles Finney was an evangelist in the 1800s whose life was a powerful example of holiness. Finney was so consecrated to God that wherever he went the manifest presence of God went with him. When Finney entered a factory, the presence and conviction of God fell on the people working there. They began to weep and repent even before he preached.

By faithfully walking in holiness before the Lord wherever he went, Charles Finney brought the glory of God with him. I believe that we today can also see such manifestations of God's glory if we live a truly holy lifestyle.

Let me offer five practical steps to help you in your commitment to walk in holiness:

1. *Be born again.* If you have not given your life to Jesus, you cannot be holy. None of us can be holy in our own strength. The Bible says that all have sinned and fallen short of the glory of God (see Romans 3:23). We need God's grace for Him to declare us as righteous, and we need His Spirit to change us from within.

2. *Seek inner healing and deliverance for persistent sin patterns.* If you are struggling with repetitive sins, get outside help. There are ministries trained in inner healing and deliverance. You do not need to live in guilt and condemnation. There are members of the Body of Christ who can help show you the way to freedom.

3. *Be continually filled with the Holy Spirit.* "Do not get drunk on wine, which leads to debauchery. Instead, be filled with the Spirit" (Ephesians 5:18). Every morning, I say to God, "Fill me afresh." Each of us needs a daily infilling of the Holy Spirit to be able to walk in love, joy, peace, patience, kindness, goodness, faithfulness, gentleness and self-control.

4. *Be faithful with daily spiritual disciplines.* "Like newborn babies, crave pure spiritual milk, so that by it you may grow up in your salvation" (1 Peter 2:2). There is no substitute for the spiritual disciplines of reading the Bible and praying. Meditating on God's Word renews our minds and keeps our ways pure (see Psalm 119:9).

5. *Seek personal accountability in the context of community.* "My brothers, if one of you should wander from the truth and someone should bring him back, remember this: Whoever turns a sinner from the error of his way will save him from death and cover over a multitude of sins" (James 5:19–20). As followers of

Christ, we need to be committed to a local church, because we need to be accountable to others and to receive discipleship and mentoring from them.

God is looking for His people to live a consecrated, holy life. He wants to release His glory through those who, like Charles Finney, will set themselves apart to Him and apart from sin. Like my friend Cindy Jacobs, I believe we will see a sweeping holiness movement take place in the Church before God releases a glory movement unlike any we have seen before. I want to be ready, to be a part of this holiness revolution when it comes. And if you are committed to being holy by God's grace, you too will see the release of His manifest glory in greater measure.

8

How to Receive More Glory

One night in March 2008, I was speaking to a packed-out Oasis Church in London. The five-hundred-seat sanctuary was standing room only. The overflow room also was completely filled with people hungry for God. In that outer overflow room sat a woman who was deaf in one ear. Believing she would be healed that night, she left her hearing aid at home.

Watching the service on the big screen, the woman could not hear the message clearly and she felt discouraged. Quietly in her heart, she cried out to God with desperation. Just as she was about to leave, the Lord gave me a word of knowledge. I said to the gathering, "There is someone here who is partially deaf. That person's ear is opening up right now."

As soon as I said those words, the woman's ear popped open. She could hear perfectly. The Lord healed her instantly! Immediately, she came into the main sanctuary to testify of the miracle she had received.

Even while sitting in a different room, watching a piped-in service on a television screen, this woman had such a hunger for God that it moved Him to give me a word of knowledge for her. And He healed her deaf ear.

God is pouring out His glory on those who are ready to receive it. We know He wants to reveal His character and goodness to us and to give us His power to release signs and wonders. Yet how do we become vessels that are prepared to receive His glory?

How Do We Receive His Glory?

I believe there are five key components to receiving more of God's glory.

1. Repent and Consecrate

The first key is repentance. In Joel 2, we see God urging His people to repent of their sins:

"Even now," declares the LORD, "return to me with all your heart, with fasting and weeping and mourning" (Joel 2:12). This verse follows later in the chapter: "And afterward, I will pour out my Spirit on all people. Your sons and daughters will prophesy, your old men will dream dreams, your young men will see visions" (Joel 2:28).

God requires His people to rend their hearts before He will pour out His Spirit. Repentance always comes before His manifest presence, His glory, is released. When we repent and turn to God, He knows we are ready to receive more of Him. And He responds by pouring Himself out upon us. Peter sums up this process in Acts 3:19: "Repent, then, and turn to God, so that your sins may be wiped out, that times of refreshing may come from the Lord."

God is looking for people who are consecrated, who will offer themselves as a living sacrifice. Some believers may not want to pay the price of consecration because it requires holiness and obedience to God's will. But the Bible says He gives the Holy Spirit to those who obey Him (see Acts 5:32). Only when we choose to repent and become, by His grace, fully consecrated to Him will He pour out His glory, revealing His goodness and power in and through our lives.

2. Hunger and Thirst

In addition to repenting and consecrating ourselves to God, we must be hungry and thirsty for more of Him. Matthew 5:6 tells us, "Blessed are those who hunger and thirst for righteousness, for they will be filled." When we are hungry for more of Him, He will fill us with more of Himself, including His glory.

Consider the story of Evan Roberts. He was a young Welshman who left work in a coal mine to study for the ministry at the turn of the twentieth century. Roberts was desperate for more of God. He gathered a group of young people around him, and together they prayed persistently for eleven years asking God to pour out His Spirit. Because of their hunger, the Holy Spirit fell powerfully in 1904, ushering in the Welsh Revival, which spread throughout the world.[1]

Many of the great revivals throughout history have been birthed because of the hunger and thirst of a few consecrated individuals in a local church. John Wesley, the forefront revivalist of the First Great Awakening of the 1700s, stated, "If you want to see revival, get on fire for God, and people will come to see you burn." It does not take a multitude of people to bring about a move of God. One person's persistent hunger for God can usher in His manifest presence.

Hunger and thirst for the Lord's presence is not only the key to starting revival, it is also the key to receiving *from* revival. In 1994, when God's Spirit was being poured out in Toronto, I attended with Lou Engle, my co-pastor at the time and one of my closest friends. As Lou and I experienced God's manifest presence there I said to him, "We're making a covenant right now to jump into this river and stay there." Because of our hunger, we made a commitment to revival. And as a result of that commitment, we tasted God's glory and experienced tremendous blessings in our lives and ministries.

One blessing I already described was the revival that began at our church, Harvest Rock, in 1995. We held protracted meetings five nights a week for over three and a half years. The covenant that Lou and I made in Toronto also birthed The Call, a youth movement that mobilized massive groups from two generations to hold days of prayer and fasting for revival. In the year 2000, over four hundred thousand young people gathered in Washington, DC, to fast and pray for the nation. The next year, some fifty thousand youth gathered in Boston, just after the September 11 tragedy. This in turn led to a gathering of almost ninety thousand in Flushing Meadows, New York, in 2002. In 2007, seventy thousand gathered in Nashville's Titan Stadium.

God honors our hunger and thirst for Him. King David gave this advice to his son Solomon: "The LORD searches every heart and understands every motive behind the thoughts. If you seek him, he will be found by you" (1 Chronicles 28:9). Our sovereign God knows our every thought and desire. If we genuinely hunger and thirst for Him and seek Him, He will pour out His Spirit on us and through us.

3. Receive an Impartation

A third key to experiencing more of God's glory is to receive an impartation from men and women of God who are being used in revival. A primary way to give or receive an impartation is through the laying on of hands.

The laying on of hands is not a new practice. It is a custom mentioned in both Testaments of the Bible. Hebrews

6:1–2 includes it as one of the elementary principles of life in Christ, along with repentance, faith, baptism, resurrection of the dead and eternal judgment. In the Old Testament, we see that Jacob laid his hands on his grandsons in order to bestow an impartation of blessing on them (see Genesis 48:14).

In the life of the early Church, the laying on of hands also played a key role. Not only did the apostles heal by the laying on of hands (see Acts 28:8), they also imparted spiritual gifts with their hands. When Peter and John placed their hands on the Samaritans in Acts 8:17, "They received the Holy Spirit." In Ephesus, "When Paul placed his hands on them, the Holy Spirit came on them, and they spoke in tongues and prophesied" (Acts 19:6).

Throughout the Bible, we see that something is transferred with the laying on of hands, whether it is blessing, healing, tongues, prophecy or a baptism of the Holy Spirit. This principle of transference through impartation continues to operate today.

I received an impartation when Rev. Billy Graham preached at the Rose Bowl in Pasadena in 2004. I had the overwhelming honor of meeting Rev. Graham with four other pastors on the Executive Committee. Before the service, I was invited to join him and these distinguished pastors of Los Angeles, Dr. Lloyd Ogilvie, Dr. Jack Hayford, and Bishop Ken Ulmer. During our meeting, I worked up the courage to ask Rev. Graham for an impartation. I was astounded by the humility in his response. He said, "I need an impartation from *you*," referring to the pastors who were around him. We each took turns laying hands on him and praying for him. Then we joined in a circle with our arms around each other as Rev. Graham prayed for God to bless each of us to be soul winners. It was a powerful moment! I was blessed to be standing next to him when he prayed for us. And I believe that I received an impartation during that time of prayer.

We see other methods of impartation in the Bible. Second Kings 13:21 states, "They threw the man's body into Elisha's tomb. When the body touched Elisha's bones, the man came to life and stood up on his feet." Even after his death, the bones of Elisha imparted the glory of the Lord.

Peter's shadow released the healing power of Christ. "People brought the sick into the streets and laid them on beds and mats so that at least Peter's shadow might fall on some of them as he passed by" (Acts 5:15). Handkerchiefs that Paul touched were effective in healing the sick and casting out demons. "God did extraordinary miracles through Paul, so that even handkerchiefs and aprons that had touched him were taken to the sick, and their illnesses were cured and the evil spirits left them" (Acts 19:11). It is clear God releases His glory in many ways. But in all these different examples, God imparts His glory through His servants, people who were carrying His anointing and power.

We can receive an impartation from God's servants, but we can also receive an impartation from the Lord by physically being in a hotspot of revival. I know a couple in ministry who took a group of people from their church to a revival. They arrived late one night, and when they got to the revival center the service was already over. One of the young women in their group had been suffering from physical pain. That night she was so intensely hungry for the Lord that she ran forward to the empty stage anyway. She was immediately hit by the power of the Holy Spirit and instantly delivered of all pain in her body.

While the examples of impartation I have just described might seem a bit fantastic and beyond our ordinary experience, they are nonetheless powerful and real. God's glory has substance. It can touch a person, rest on an object, and fill a place. It is as real and available to us today as it was in the early Church, for God wants to pour His glory upon us. Receiving an impartation—whether through the laying on of hands or attending a hotspot of revival—is a significant way to receive more of God's glory.

4. Give It Away

This extremely important key is one that is too often overlooked. God loves and wants to abundantly bless us, but His glory is not just for us to receive and keep. It is also for us to give away. Once we have received His glory, it is important that we pray for people, preach the Gospel of the Kingdom and heal the sick and cast out demons in the name of Jesus (see Mark 16:15–20). God's glory is for the harvest. Revival begins with the church, but when we take His glory beyond the church and into the community, the spiritual blindness of unbelievers is lifted. They begin to see and understand God's goodness and are attracted to Him.

For us to take God's glory outside the four walls of the church means we will take signs and wonders into the communities we live in. I support all forms of evangelism, including evangelism in the traditional sense of preaching the Gospel. I believe the Gospel in itself is the power of God for salvation (see Romans 1:16). But I also firmly believe we are commanded to take God's glory into our communities by releasing His presence and His power through signs, wonders and prophecy.

For over 2,000 years we have been praying the Lord's Prayer, "Your kingdom come, your will be done on earth as it is in heaven" (Matthew 6:10). We desire His Kingdom and glory to come. And Jesus Himself tells us, "If I drive out demons by the Spirit of God, then the kingdom of God has come upon you" (Matthew 12:28). If signs and wonders do not follow the Gospel we preach, then we are preaching only part of the Gospel. There is more to the Gospel than salvation from sin. The full Gospel includes baptism in the Spirit, speaking in tongues and the release of signs and wonders, such as healing

111

and deliverance. God wants His Kingdom, His power and His glory to accompany the Gospel wherever we go!

Being ready to share the Gospel in any of these ways is a key to receiving more of God's glory. Jesus said, "Whoever can be trusted with very little can also be trusted with much" (Luke 16:10). If we are faithful with what He has already given us, He will give us more.

Recently I was in the waiting area of a new carwash when I noticed a woman wearing a neck brace. The Lord spoke to me, "That wasn't because of a car accident. She has a disease." When God gives you a word of knowledge, especially one that is that specific, it is important to steward it and act upon it. I knew I was supposed to pray for the woman.

I sat down next to her and prayed silently, "Lord, please open the door for me to share the Gospel with her and pray for her." As soon as I finished the prayer, she initiated a conversation, asking me, "How do you like this new carwash?"

"I don't know. It's my second time here," I answered. Then I asked, "What happened to your neck?"

She said, "I was sitting on a chair, leaning back, and I fell and hurt my neck. It wasn't a big fall, but my neck didn't get better. I went to the chiropractor and to the doctor, and they said there weren't any broken bones. But it started to get worse. I was in excruciating pain and my left arm started to go numb. I went back to the doctor to get an MRI, and they found that I have a bone disease. It's causing my neck to deteriorate."

This confirmed the word of knowledge that the Lord had given me. I said to the woman, "I'm a pastor in this city. May I pray for you?"

"Yes," she said immediately. Some believers hesitate to pray for strangers, thinking they will refuse prayer. But in my experience, people who are desperate for healing seldom refuse prayer, whether they are Christians or not. All we need to do is step out in faith, and God will do the rest.

I prayed for her while the other people in the waiting area watched. My prayer was simple: "Father, in the name of Jesus, I ask that by Your power, You heal her completely." Then I told her to act upon the prayer and do something to test the healing. "Begin to move your neck," I suggested. "Do something you couldn't do before."

She moved her neck, tested it, and said, "You know what? I don't feel any pain!" She was incredulous. Lifting her left arm with ease, she exclaimed, "There's no more numbness!"

It was amazing. I said to her, "Jesus has given you a wonderful gift today. Would you like to give your heart to Him?"

"Yes!" she exclaimed. She gave her heart to the Lord there in the carwash waiting area.

This is what God wants us to do. We are to take His glory outside the four walls of the church—to our work, our school, a restaurant, even a carwash, wherever! When we give His glory away, we open ourselves to receive more from Him.

5. Build the Church

The fifth key component to receiving more glory is to build the church. God's glory is not meant only for us to soak up and enjoy for ourselves. His glory is released for a larger purpose. As the early Church experienced Pentecost in Acts 2, they devoted themselves to the apostles' teachings, breaking of bread, fellowship and prayer (see Acts 2:42). They continued building the Church in the midst of an incredible revival.

The earliest Christians met from house to house. We know they were able to go from glory to glory because Acts 4:31 says they were filled with the Holy Spirit again, after their initial filling in Acts 2. At the same time, they were able to grow in size. "The Lord added to their number daily those who were being saved" (Acts 2:47). Why did they receive another infilling of the Holy Spirit and grow in number? They were building the church in the midst of revival.

If pastored correctly, revival builds the Church. But this is not easily done. In fact, when mishandled a revival's fire can extinguish with little or no lasting impact. In 1994, when the Holy Spirit fell on Toronto, I saw two different streams of people who received from that revival and brought it back to their churches. On one end, there were those who did not understand the purpose of the revival; they brought back to their churches an excitement that did not last. In fact, some churches that were major revival centers then no longer exist today. On the other end, there were churches that received an impartation of revival, held protracted meetings, and continued to grow at the same time. These churches are thriving today.

This was a trend in earlier revivals as well. Calvary Chapel, which emerged from the Jesus People Movement, remains strong today. Aimee Semple McPherson, who started the Foursquare denomination, built her church in addition to holding healing services. Today Foursquare churches number in the tens of thousands around the world.

In 1995, before John Arnott and I left the Vineyard church movement, John Wimber called us to give us advice concerning the revival we were then experiencing. One thing he said stood out powerfully to me. It was simple but easy to overlook amid all the excitement. He implored us: "Build the Church." He advised us to keep structures in place to maintain small groups, and to hold Sunday school. We followed his advice, because we knew John himself was successful in growing the Vineyard denomination while hosting an earlier revival in the 1980s.

Jesus emphasized the building of the Church when He said, "I will build my church, and the gates of Hades will not overcome it" (Matthew 16:18). Whenever He manifests His glory by pouring out His Spirit, God is giving us the greatest blessing as He builds His Church.

More Glory

These five components—repentance and consecration, hunger and thirst, impartation, giving it away and building the Church—are practical keys to receiving more of God's glory. I have learned these keys as a result of being used in revival for the past 14 years, and I still follow these principles today.

I thank God that I have been used in revival, and by His grace, I want to continually be used in revival. I want to be like Rev. Billy Graham, who carries revival with him, filling the Rose Bowl in Pasadena at age 87. As soon as he stepped into the pulpit, God's anointing came, and the Holy Spirit filled the stadium. Rev. Graham is my hero and example.

In our church, we have a saying: "Refirement, not retirement." No matter how much glory we have received or how powerfully God has used us, we can always experience more of our Lord and Savior. The glory of our Lord is eternal, ever increasing and everlasting.

9

From Glory to Glory

Throughout history the church has experienced waves of God's glory. We know that God is omnipresent, that His presence is always with us. But the glory I am referring to is His manifest presence, through which He reveals His goodness or displays His power through signs and wonders.

Today, we call this revival. I believe that the Holy Spirit is sovereign in determining the release of revival. Yet as we discussed in the previous chapter, I also believe we have the potential to call on God, to bring about His kingdom through prayer and our hunger for Him. The church has seen revival happen this way throughout the centuries.

Repeatedly, God has poured out wave after wave of His Spirit almost like clockwork. Consider these examples from the latter half of the past century:

- 1948 saw the beginning of the Latter Rain revival in Canada. Many healing evangelists were united and launched under Gordon Lindsey and the Voice of Healing movement. These included Oral Roberts and William Branham.

- 1958 saw another visitation, upon Dennis Bennett in Van Nuys, California. This led to the beginning of the Charismatic movement.
- In 1967 revival came with the Jesus People Movement, led by Chuck Smith and Calvary Chapel. Reaching new heights in 1971, the movement made the cover of *Time* magazine.
- From 1982 to 1986, John Wimber and his groundbreaking class at Fuller Seminary—on "Signs, Wonders, and Church Growth at the Anaheim Vineyard"—brought another wave of glory. Peter Wagner called this movement the "Third Wave" of a century-long revival. In Wagner's thinking, the first wave was the Azusa Street Revival of 1906, the second wave was the Charismatic Renewal of 1958, which continued into the Jesus People revival, and the third wave was the movement that began with John Wimber in the 1980s.

Because God brings wave after wave of His glory, releasing His goodness and power, it is possible for us to ride each wave of revival until the next. In fact, as we shall see, it is God's will for us to go from glory to glory.

A Biblical Principle Concerning Glory

I want to explore a principle in Scripture that speaks of God's people moving from glory to glory. This passage specifically refers to personal transformation, but it contains a principle that we can also apply to revival:

If the ministry that brought death, which was engraved in letters on stone, came with glory, so that the Israelites could not look steadily at the face of Moses because of its glory, fading though it was, will not the ministry of the Spirit be even more glorious? If the ministry that condemns men is glorious, how much more glorious is the ministry that brings righteousness! For what was glorious has no glory now in comparison with the surpassing glory. And if what was fading away came with glory, how much greater is the glory of that which lasts!

2 Corinthians 3:7–11

The "ministry that brought death" that Paul refers to here is the ministry under the law of the Ten Commandments. The Commandments alone cannot save us. We will be lost if we try to obey them on our own, without relying on the grace of God. And yet the law itself is glorious. God's glory accompanied the actual revelation of the Commandments, for in the moment the Lord revealed the law to Moses, He released His glory in a tangible way. God's manifest presence was so powerful that the children of Israel could not look steadily on Moses' face because of the glory he carried following his encounter with the Lord. The people had to cover his face with a veil. Yet even Moses' glowing countenance eventually faded. The glory of God—the actual, tangible presence of the Lord—literally rested on Moses' face, but over time it passed away. I want to compare this glory, described so vividly in this example from the Old Covenant, to what we have in the New Covenant with Christ.

Paul also refers in this passage to the "ministry of the Spirit," which is more glorious than the "ministry that brought death" (meaning the law). Since Pentecost, under the New Covenant, God has poured out His Spirit on *all* flesh—not just on *one* person named Moses—and those who tap into it can receive His glory. So if Moses, an Old Testament prophet, had glory, then the ministry of righteousness—which comes in God's New Covenant with us through Jesus Christ—should exceed the Old Covenant ministry in its measure of glory.

In referring to the New Covenant obtained in Christ's victory over sin and death, Paul states, "God made him who had no sin to be sin for us, so that in him we might become the righteousness of God" (2 Corinthians 5:21). We are all made righteous through the blood of Jesus Christ when we accept Him as our Lord and Savior. And we now have the potential to walk in greater glory than Moses did because we have access to this greater New Covenant.

Paul concludes the passage with an amazing verse: "And we, who with unveiled faces all reflect the Lord's glory, are being transformed into his likeness with ever-increasing glory, which comes from the Lord, who is the Spirit" (2 Corinthians 3:18).

God's principle is for us to go from glory to glory, being transformed into the image of Christ. I believe this means He wants us to immerse ourselves in every single wave of revival until He comes back or until we go home to be with Him. Jesus tells us, "God gives the Spirit without limit" (John 3:34). This means God gives us His Spirit without holding back. In fact, His will is for the whole earth to be full of His glory. To this end, He promises that His glory will fill the earth, and that He will pour out His Spirit on all flesh: "The earth will be filled with the knowledge of the glory of the Lord, as the waters cover the sea" (Habakkuk 2:14).

I have firsthand experience with the life-transforming power of God's manifest glory in a revival context. I was saved through the Jesus People Movement. The church I pastor, Harvest Rock, was birthed in revival through the Toronto outpouring. Since then I have committed myself to continue experiencing the unique encounter with God that is contained in each new revival, wherever it breaks out around the world.

The Restorative Power of Each Wave

As I look back through the history of revival, I see that every wave of God's outpouring is important because, in each revival, He restores something. In fact, over the past half-century, we see that in each movement God restored an office within the five-fold ministry, including apostles, prophets, evangelists, pastors and teachers.

For example, in 1948 God brought forth evangelism in a new way, notably through Billy Graham but also through healing evangelists such as A. A. Allen, Jack Coe, Oral Roberts, William Branham, T. L. Osborn and others. In 1958, the Church saw the rise of pastors who boldly proclaimed and operated in a charismatic Gospel, such as Dennis Bennett (Charismatic Anglican), Larry Christianson (Charismatic Lutheran) and Gerald Derstine (Charismatic Mennonite) to mention a few. In 1967, in response to another move of God, the ministry of anointed teachers became predominant. This included teachers such as Chuck Smith, Kenneth Copeland, Jack Hayford, Derek Prince and many others. (Derek Prince was part of a group of leaders that became known as "The Teachers," based in Fort Lauderdale, Florida.)

In the "Third Wave" of the 1980s, God brought forth prophets, as John Wimber introduced the "Kansas City prophets" Paul Cain, Mike Bickle, Bob Jones, James Goll and Jill Austin. Other prophets also emerged during that period, including my friend and covenant brother Lou Engle, my sister in the Lord Cindy Jacobs, Jane Hamon and Chuck Pierce. The 1994 revival in Toronto restored the office of the apostle with the birth of many apostolic networks, including John and Carol Arnott's Partners in Harvest, Rick Joyner's MorningStar, Bill Johnson's Global Legacy, Heidi and Rolland Baker's Iris Ministries and our church's own Harvest International Ministry.

Now, in 2009, we see the convergence of all five of these restored offices coming together and being expressed through the Body of Christ in His followers the saints. Ordinary lay people are being equipped to move in signs and wonders, to evangelize, to teach, to plant churches, to prophesy and to preach. It is catapulting the people of God to do His work in establishing the Kingdom. Each wave of revival has been significant in its fulfillment of God's purposes, to see His glory fill the earth and His Spirit poured out on all flesh.

The Fullness of Glory

Unfortunately, every wave of revival has its critics. And, sadly, often the leaders of a previous move of God are the ones who most criticize the leaders of God's next wave. But in order to go from glory to glory, we must stay teachable, walk in humility and remain willing to receive what God is doing in each revival. God's ways are not our ways, and if we think we know it all or have experienced it all, we operate under a religious spirit that is displeasing to God.

I learned this important lesson during the 1980s. I missed the revival with John Wimber, even though I had been saved and baptized in the Holy Spirit during the Jesus People Movement. When revival came to the Anaheim Vineyard, I had arrogance in my heart. I was a student at Fuller Seminary in Pasadena at the time. Peter Wagner, who was a professor there, suggested that I enroll in John Wimber's class on "Signs, Wonders and Church Growth," which I did. But when I saw the signs and wonders taking place in the class, I told myself, "I've seen all this before."

As a young Christian, I had overseen the healing room ministry for a group called TAG in Washington, D.C. After five years watching healings occur there, the types of miracles I saw at Fuller were nothing new to me. But having that kind of attitude is dangerous. I found out it is possible to become immune to revival. When you taste a little bit of it, you may think you've already been exposed to everything there is about that revival. You can become blinded to the significance of what God is actually doing. A "been there, done that, got the T-shirt" attitude can be detrimental, preventing us from experiencing the fullness of what God wants to give us.

Instead of being arrogant or passive, we should keep humble and contrite hearts before God. I believe that if I had been more receptive to God's revival at the Vineyard, I would not have experienced as many hardships in my ministry and personal life during the 1980s and early 1990s. I thank God I learned from my mistake, and I didn't hesitate to plunge into the next glory wave when God poured out His Spirit in Toronto. By His grace, I have stayed in that river of revival ever since.

Now, when a new revival breaks out, my mentality is no longer, "I've seen this before. It is nothing new." Instead, I position myself to receive more. My mentality is, "Here's another wave. I want to saturate myself in the unique glory it brings. I want to ride it to the next wave, and the next wave after that." I have committed myself to staying in the glory river of revival, from wave to wave, until Jesus comes again or He takes me home.

Second Chronicles 16:9 says, "The eyes of the LORD range throughout the earth to strengthen those whose hearts are fully committed to him." If we increase in our hunger for God and our consecration to Him, the Lord will manifest His glory in and through our lives. He wants us to go from glory to glory, until we receive the fullness of His glory and are changed into the image of Jesus Christ.

Why not be a walking vessel of revival for the rest of your life? You are a carrier of His glory! Be a carrier of revival to your generation and to generations to come, as long as the Lord tarries. Amen!

10

The Glory of God and Apostolic Alignment

In his book *In the Day of Thy Power*, Arthur Wallis gives us this counsel: "If you would make the greatest success of your life, try to discover what God is doing in your time and fling yourself into the accomplishment of His purpose and will."[1]

If we are to do what is best, both for our lives and for the Kingdom of God, we need to find out what the Lord is doing in our generation and commit our lives to fulfilling it. How do we prepare for what the Spirit is about to do? One way we can do this is by bringing proper apostolic alignment to the Body of Christ. In this chapter, we'll see why this must happen before any major societal transformation occurs in the world. Our own house must first be in order and in unity. Proper apostolic alignment brings forth God's commanded blessing, beginning first in His house and from there, flowing out into society.

The Apostle and the High Priest

Before we can address proper apostolic alignment in the Church today, we must understand the parallel between alignment in the offices of the high priest in the Old Testament and the apostle in the New Testament.

David beautifully describes the principle of alignment under the Old Testament high priest:

> How good and pleasant it is when brothers live together in unity! It is like precious oil poured on the head, running down on the beard, running down on Aaron's beard, down upon the collar of his robes. It is as if the dew of Hermon were falling on Mount Zion. For there the LORD bestows his blessing, even life forevermore.
>
> Psalm 133:1–3

David clearly states that God's people abide under His blessing when they move in unity, functioning as one. We need to understand that David is referring to a special kind of unity. Let me explain within the context of this psalm.

Aaron served as Israel's high priest during the time of his brother, Moses. In Psalm 133, the oil came upon Aaron, who represented the office of high priest, and flowed from top to bottom—from Aaron's head, down his beard and to the lower edge of his robes. David compares this to the dew falling on Mount Hermon and flowing down to Zion. It is no accident that David refers to Mount Hermon in the passage. Just where is Mount Hermon? Geographically, it is at the head, or top, of Israel. It is also where the dew falls first. The water flows down from there, to Mount Zion and the rest of Israel.

In this passage, David uses two examples of a downward flow to illustrate the principle of alignment the Lord wants us to understand. When David mentions Aaron in this psalm, he is referring to an alignment under the high priest. The oil symbolizes God's favor and blessings, and it flowed from the high priest downward to the rest of the people. Through this imagery David is telling us that when we come into God's delegated alignment, we will start to experience His favor and blessing.

What does this passage have to do with proper apostolic alignment in the Church today? The high priest in the Old Testament served the same role in God's house that the apostle does in the New Testament. We find this explained in the book of Hebrews.

The writer states, "Therefore, holy brothers, who share in the heavenly calling, fix your thoughts on Jesus, the apostle and high priest whom we confess" (Hebrews 3:1). Both titles are ascribed to Jesus here. He is both the ultimate apostle and the ultimate high priest. As the apostle, Jesus represents the New Covenant, and as the high priest, He represents the Old Covenant. This parallel is helpful—and important—when reading Hebrews, because the book discusses the better covenant we now have in Christ. Alignment in the Old Covenant under the high priest was good, but now, under the New Covenant, Jesus has established a better order. This new order includes the five-fold ministry offices of apostles, prophets, pastors, evangelists and teachers.

With the New Covenant, we are no longer under the leadership of high priests. Yet we are now called to apostolic alignment—that is, to be under the leadership of the apostles, prophets, evangelists, pastors and teachers whom God has gifted and appointed over His church. Ephesians 4:11 says God has given us apostles and prophets until we attain "to the whole measure of the fullness of Christ" (Ephesians 4:11–13). Clearly, the Church has yet to attain that full measure. In no place does the Bible say the offices and ministries of apostles and prophets have ceased to exist or function. In fact, they are described as foundational to the Church. Paul says in

Ephesians 2:20 that the Church is "built on the foundation of the apostles and prophets, with Christ Jesus himself as the chief cornerstone." Again, the order is important: first apostles and second prophets. Another key passage is 1 Corinthians 12:28: "In the church God has appointed first of all apostles, second prophets, third teachers, then workers of miracles." Peter Wagner, in his 2008 book *Dominion*, writes, "The numbering is not simply a random selection. Although it does not imply a hierarchy, it is clearly a divine order. Apostles are first and prophets are second. All the other gifts will function to their fullest potential only if they are properly related to apostles and prophets."[2]

Jesus selected twelve apostles, but the New Testament makes clear that the office of apostle was not exclusive to the original disciples of Christ. Other apostles are mentioned throughout the New Testament, including Andronicus and Junias (see Romans 16:7), Silas and Timothy (see 1 Thessalonians 1:1, 6), and James (see Galatians 1:18–19). This indicates that the office of apostle multiplied as the Church grew.

The word "apostle" appears 76 times in the New Testament, more than any other office. This may seem surprising, because we tend to emphasize pastoral leadership in the Church today. But the word for "pastor" and its synonyms are mentioned in the New Testament 67 times. I believe it is significant that the New Testament focuses more on apostolic activities, revelation and teachings than on the functions of any other office in the early Church.

Apostolic Alignment

The Greek word in the Bible for "alignment" is *katartismos*. It means: "to properly align or set in original order," the way a doctor might reset a broken bone. The word appears in

Paul's list of five-fold ministry offices mentioned in Ephesians 4:11–12: "He Himself gave some to be apostles, some prophets, some evangelists, and some pastors and teachers, for the equipping [*katartismos*] of the saints for the work of the ministry, for the edifying of the body of Christ" (NKJV). Paul is telling us that the various ministry offices, when working together properly, help align or set in right order the Church. In this way Christ's Body is built up to proclaim the Gospel and advance the Kingdom.

In the Old Testament, before the coming of Jesus, God's blessings flowed down to the people of Israel when they were aligned under the leadership of the high priest. God blesses His children similarly today, when we properly align ourselves under the leadership of the apostles He has chosen.

Throughout Scripture we see that being in proper alignment in our relationships brings a blessing. Paul writes in Ephesians 6:1–3 that God instituted a proper alignment when He established the family: "Children, obey your parents in the Lord, for this is right. 'Honor your father and mother'— which is the first commandment with a promise—'that it may go well with you and that you may enjoy long life on the earth.'" Paul makes clear that when we are in proper alignment with regard to our family, God bestows blessings upon us so that things may go well with us and that we may enjoy long lives.

The same is true with proper apostolic alignment in the Church. When this is in place, God commands His blessings to flow. In his book, *The Supernatural Ways of Royalty*, Kris Vallotton, Senior Associate Pastor of Bethel Church in Redding, California, candidly speaks about his covenant commitment to the church's Senior Pastor, Bill Johnson. The Lord showed Kris that though he often emphasized being in a covenant of proper alignment, he had not entered into that commitment with his own senior "father" in the Lord.

Conviction grew within Kris until one day he said to Bill, "I covenant to spend the rest of my life serving you."[3]

Kris says this commitment had a powerful impact on him: "Those words have changed my life. I have come into a whole new level in God since then. My ministry has doubled, and my finances have more than doubled."[4] Because of the apostolic alignment in the leadership and congregation of Bethel Church, God has poured out his blessing and favor on the members, the church, the city of Redding and even its neighboring cities. People travel from all over the world to encounter the manifest presence of God in that church. In addition, the city has prospered. Bill Johnson recently told me that Redding is one of the few cities in California that has not been as dramatically impacted by the economic downturn that began in the United States in September 2008, compared to other cities in California. My observation is that every time I go to speak at Bethel, it seems the city has grown and prospered. I believe Redding will be one of the most transformed cities in the days and years ahead.

We see through Kris's example how God's blessing is poured out when His people are properly aligned. This type of alignment in covenant relationships is not a mindless obedience to an authority figure. It is a willingness to honor the leadership of authority we recognize as placed over us by God. Obviously, not everyone is called to make a lifetime covenant like the one Kris made to Bill Johnson. What is important is the principle of alignment under the direction of the Holy Spirit. It involves voluntarily entering into a cooperative partnership where we work together with leadership because we recognize the divine purpose in our joint calling and our spiritual accountability with each other. We further our joint efforts by choosing to defend one another, and though at times we may challenge one another, we never criticize or speak evil of each other. We each remain responsible for our conduct and individual decisions, but we are committed to building each other up, not seeking our own way.

This blessing of proper apostolic authority applies to ministries as well as to individual believers. As an example of this principle, a few years ago our church commissioned a pastoral couple, John and Michele Park, to plant a church in Diamond Bar, California, under our apostolic authority. John and Michele readily aligned themselves with our leadership, and God abundantly blessed their fledgling ministry. One example of this blessing was God's provision to them of a building that was perfect in size and already set up for ministry. Its previous tenant was a congregation that had remodeled the church with state-of-the-art equipment but had quickly outgrown the physical space. Now, because that church's lease was up and they were moving on, John and Michele's congregation was able to transition smoothly into the building. It was like moving into a model home with free furniture thrown in by the developer! I believe this blessing and favor happened in part because the Parks' ministry and church were apostolically aligned.

Alignment Promotes Unity and Brings God's Glory

Proper apostolic alignment causes the church to operate in unity, and God blesses it with visitations of His glory. Consider this passage:

> The trumpeters and singers joined in unison, as with one voice, to give praise and thanks to the LORD. Accompanied by trumpets, cymbals and other instruments, they raised their voices in praise to the LORD and sang: "He is good; his love endures forever." Then the temple of the LORD was filled with a cloud, and the priests could not perform their service because of the cloud, for the glory of the LORD filled the temple of God.
>
> 2 Chronicles 5:13–14

What an incredible scene! At the dedication of the Temple, everyone was in alignment and all was in order. These trumpeters and singers weren't just playing and singing the same tune; they were in such unity that they played and sang as if they had one voice and one heart. They were completely unified as they praised the Lord. Then the Lord filled the Temple with a cloud of His manifest glory, and it was so strong that the priests could not perform their service. God honored their unity with His glorious manifest presence.

This is not an isolated incident in Scripture. We see in the New Testament an example of how alignment and unity brought God's glory at Pentecost. In Acts 2 we read that the Lord poured His Spirit on the disciples, yet it is important to note what took place before that day.

Jesus appeared to a number of people after his resurrection. In 1 Corinthians 15:6, the apostle Paul states that Jesus appeared to over five hundred of the brethren at one time. The event and place are not described, but since Paul refers to them as "the brethren," I think we can assume that they were followers of Christ. In Acts 1, Jesus appeared to His disciples, commanding them, "Do not leave Jerusalem, but wait for the gift my Father promised, which you have heard me speak about" (Acts 1:4). The disciples obeyed and were joined by the women, His mother Mary, family members and others, totaling about 120 people. It is highly likely that some of these 120 were from the five hundred brethren to whom Jesus had appeared earlier. Of these disciples, only 120 obeyed His command. These were the ones who decided to pay the price, gathering in prayer and waiting. And it was the apostles who led the group in the Upper Room as they awaited the fulfillment of Jesus' words:

> Then they returned to Jerusalem from the hill called the Mount of Olives, a Sabbath day's walk from the city. When they arrived, they went upstairs to the room where they

were staying. Those present were Peter, John, James and Andrew; Philip and Thomas, Bartholomew and Matthew; James son of Alphaeus and Simon the Zealot, and Judas son of James. They all joined together constantly in prayer, along with the women and Mary the mother of Jesus, and with his brothers.

Acts 1:12–14

Scripture indicates that these disciples were in constant prayer and unity. I don't think it is just by accident that Luke names each of the apostles specifically with the 120. I believe it was this apostolic alignment and unity that led to a release of glory through the Holy Spirit:

When the day of Pentecost came, they were all together in one place. Suddenly a sound like the blowing of a violent wind came from heaven and filled the whole house where they were sitting. They saw what seemed to be tongues of fire that separated and came to rest on each of them. All of them were filled with the Holy Spirit and began to speak in other tongues as the Spirit enabled them.

Acts 2:1–4

At Pentecost, the Holy Spirit descended on a room that was unified, with the disciples in one accord and in one place. They had obeyed the command of Jesus in Acts 1, praying together in unity day after day. God saw their obedience to His Son, their hunger for the Spirit, and their unity with each other. And His glory descended on them, blessing them by filling them all with the Spirit. In this instance, apostolic alignment and unity brought not only favor and blessing but also the glory of God in His remarkable manifest presence.

While unity brings God's glory, we also need His glory to help us *become* unified. Jesus prayed to the Father, "I

133

have given them the glory that you gave me, that they may be one as we are one: I in them, and you in me. May they be brought to complete unity to let the world know that you sent me and have loved them even as you have loved me" (John 17:22–23). Here Jesus refers to the alignment between first Himself and the Father and second Himself and us. Unity is important to God. And when we seek proper alignment, God releases His glory so that we may become one with each other, just as Jesus and the Father are one.

As we walk in unity and alignment, God pours out more of His glory on us. We must never forget that our power is greatly increased when we are aligned and walk in unity. Scripture tells us, "Five of you will chase a hundred, and a hundred of you will chase ten thousand, and your enemies will fall by the sword before you" (Leviticus 26:8). When we are properly aligned, we become unified and more powerful, victorious and effective for God's Kingdom purposes.

Steps for Alignment

Here are three steps for God's people to become apostolically aligned.

1. Receive Salvation

To be properly apostolically aligned, we must first be aligned with Jesus Christ. This means putting ourselves under His loving Lordship. When we receive salvation, we receive Jesus as our Lord and Savior. And because Jesus is our Lord, we must submit everything in our lives to His authority. Relinquishing control over our individual bodies, souls and spirits to Christ puts our lives into the hands of a loving Lord who desires only good things for His children. Psalm 34:8 says, "Taste and see that the LORD is good."

2. Commit to a Local Church

In order to be properly aligned, it is also important for us to be committed to a local church. We cannot say that we are committed to Jesus if we refuse to be committed to His Body. The Bible has more than fifty "one another" verses that we cannot fulfill unless we are part of a community. These include: love one another (see John 13:34–35), be devoted to one another (see Romans 12:10), rejoice with one another (see Romans 12:15), pray for one another (see James 5:16), bear one another's burdens (see Galatians 5:13), submit to one another (see Ephesians 5:21) and fellowship with one another (see 1 John 1:7).

At times it may seem easier not to commit to a church, but God blesses those who obey Him. The Lord is a covenant maker and commands us to be people of covenant relationships. He honors our commitment to align ourselves with a community of believers through our mutual submission to each other, dedication to service together and openness to accountability with one another. As we obey His Word in this way, encouraging and bearing with one another, we grow in unity, and God blesses us by pouring out His glory on us.

There is no such thing as a perfect church, because every church is made up of humans, all of whom "fall short of the glory of God" (Romans 3:23). Moreover, not all churches carry the same anointing or are called to the same type of ministry. Just as the tribes in Israel had different strengths and functions (Levi was the priestly tribe, Judah the messianic tribe, etc.), churches are called to fulfill different purposes in the Body of Christ. We need to understand and align ourselves with a church whose values, mission and purpose correspond to our own spiritual DNA. When that correspondence is missing, it will become difficult for us to commit to alignment. It will be a forced fit and we will not feel at home.

We need to find our tribe, the community that resonates with us. Yet we must avoid getting caught up in a never-ending search for the right church. Too many Christians today wander from one temporary dwelling to another. They become "cruising charismatics," always looking for the next conference, the next opportunity for a "spiritual feeding frenzy," hooked on spiritual experiences, but avoiding any lasting commitment. God calls us to the joys, frustrations and disciplines of being planted in a community. He calls us to covenant with each other, knowing that we learn alignment and how to dwell in unity only as we live in ongoing community with other believers. In His own eternal triune Godhead, He is a community living in perfect alignment and unity, and thus becomes our perfect model.

3. Carry the Leader's Heart

Finally, to be apostolically aligned we must carry the heart of our pastor or apostle. As I stated earlier, this is not submission to some heavy-handed authority. It does not mean we are to walk in uniformity with leadership, or always be in complete agreement. Nor does it mean becoming "cookie-cutter Christians" who act, think, talk and dress alike. There is room and, indeed, *need* for diversity in our alignment and unity. In fact, times of disagreement are when our alignment is most deeply tested. We do not commit ourselves to blind obedience, but to honoring our mutual values and mission above our temporary conflicts.

Carrying the heart of our leaders also means committing to an attitude of honoring them as fathers and mothers in the faith. The writer of Hebrews says, "Obey your leaders and submit to their authority. They keep watch over you as men who must give an account. Obey them so that their work will be a joy, not a burden, for that would be of no advantage to you" (Hebrews 13:17). If we do this, God will pour out His glory upon His church beyond measure.

Apostolic alignment and unity of the body release God's blessings and favor to flow powerfully into our lives. Just as Israel aligned under Aaron the high priest and saw the glory of God, I believe God's people today, aligned in unity under His current apostles, will see God's glory descend in even greater measure.

11

The Glory of God
and Transformation

When the glory of God invades people's souls, it leads both to personal and to societal transformation. As we look back over the last few hundred years, we see that many periods of dramatic social change were preceded by an outpouring of God's glory in revival.

Revival and Reformation

The Great Awakening

The Great Awakening was a time of powerful revival in England in the 1730s. This movement of God ignited a number of revival ministries, most notably those of John and Charles Wesley and George Whitefield. Through Whitefield, the movement spread to America, where it was advanced by the fiery preaching of Jonathan Edwards[1] in Northampton, Massachusetts. In England, thousands of people came to salvation through the itinerant ministry of the Wesley brothers. Among these converts was a young man named William Wilberforce, who became a member of Parliament.

Following his conversion, Wilberforce met John Newton, the former slave ship captain who also had been converted to Christ (and who in deep repentance wrote the famous hymn "Amazing Grace"). Wilberforce was deeply moved by Newton's brutally honest accounts of the incredible human abuse in the slave trade.[2] The young politician dedicated the next 26 years of his life in Parliament to lobbying for England to stop slavery. His efforts finally resulted in the nonviolent, radical transformation of English society, as slavery was completely abolished.[3] An excellent recent motion picture, *Amazing Grace*, depicts Wilberforce's relentless efforts to change the heart of his nation through the use of its legislative process. I highly recommend this film; its story is a wonderful example of how personal revival leads to societal reformation.

The Second Great Awakening

The Second Great Awakening, which took place in America, began around 1800 on the east coast and on the western frontier of Kentucky. This movement of God also ignited several powerful societal transformations. Timothy Dwight, president of Yale and grandson of revivalist Jonathan Edwards, strongly and publicly encouraged all Christians to pursue God with all their hearts. His rhetoric, reminiscent of his famous grandfather, stirred many Yale students, including Samuel Mills.[4] Mills later transferred to Williams College in Massachusetts, taking his newfound zeal for the Lord with him. There, Mills formed a group with four other students, who covenanted with him to pray daily for their fellow students.

The young men usually met outdoors, but one day in 1801, a severe thunderstorm broke out. The group found refuge in a haystack, and while praying together there, God birthed in their spirits the desire to begin a student missionary movement in order to evangelize the world. History has dubbed this event the "Haystack Revival." Out of this vision, the first foreign missions board was established in 1810. When several workers were sent to Asia, the American missionary movement officially began.[5]

Even as Dwight was delivering his message on the east coast, a mighty outpouring of God's glory occurred in Cane Ridge, Kentucky. Initially held in churches, this revival fire spread so rapidly that soon meetings were held in fields and continued for days at a time. At its height, the Cane Ridge Revival was attracting crowds of 20,000 to a single meeting. The meetings were interdenominational, and it was common to have multiple platforms set up in the fields with seven or more ministers preaching at a time. Because there was no amplification, the people gathered around the platform of the nearest preacher.

The common thread in this revival was the outpouring of the Holy Spirit, which was often marked by dramatic manifestations. People were knocked over, seemingly unconscious, or were unable to move or jerked violently. Others were overcome with laughter and acted drunk, while still others wept or wailed. The revival attracted many visitors, and significant press coverage heightened awareness about it. Because of this revival, multitudes throughout the young nation were moved to reconsider the place of God in their lives.[6]

CHARLES FINNEY

One such person affected was Charles Finney, a young man who had been raised largely without religion. He became convinced that he needed to know the truth about how to make his soul right with God. But Finney wasn't sure he could trust traditional religion and he didn't want to be misled. So one day he took a Bible, walked into the woods and swore he would not return until his heart was right with God. He experienced a powerful conversion that day, including the baptism in the Holy Spirit—even though he had never heard of it before!

Finney went on to become one of the most influential revivalists of the period, preaching to thousands throughout the northeast. He delivered a powerful Gospel that emphasized active individual choice in salvation, seeing each person as responsible for accepting or rejecting Christ. The message he preached extended beyond salvation, encouraging people to contribute to society by focusing their Christian values on improving the quality of life for others.[7]

THE ABOLITIONIST MOVEMENT

As more people were converted, they were encouraged to actively take part in shaping their country's values and morals. Soon, increasing numbers of citizens expressed concern about the practice of slavery. Many became convinced slavery was not only dehumanizing and abusive, it was also morally wrong in the eyes of God. An abolitionist movement began to form.

By the late 1850s, the abolitionist movement had grown in number and voice and seemed headed toward a critical tipping point. No one could have foreseen that a crucial element in this tipping point would be a humble prayer meeting. In 1858, a relatively unknown businessman named Jeremiah Lamphier felt led by the Lord to start a prayer meeting for businessmen in New York City. Lamphier rented a building, passed out fliers and began to hold noon meetings in New York's business district.

The first day six people attended. Their number grew to twenty by the end of the first week, then to forty by the end of the month. The group had no set agenda but prayed as they were led by the Spirit. After the first month the group exploded in size. Within six months the movement had grown so rapidly that ten thousand businessmen were meeting in small prayer groups all over New York City and the surrounding communities. Two years later, over one million people had been converted and had joined churches throughout New England. As these growing congregations began demanding an end to slavery, the critical tipping point of the abolitionist movement was reached. This momentum eventually led to the Civil War and the emancipation of slaves.[8]

I have shared all these stories because they illustrate how God's glory transforms the world. As God transforms individual lives, those individuals, in turn, transform society. The purpose of God's glory is not to turn us into isolationists, hidden away in our church communities as if they were "Christian ghettos." God intends His glory to flow to us, in us and then through us to the world. God loves the world and wants to reestablish His Kingdom here. He desires to pour out His goodness and bless all of humankind. And He entrusts to us the ministry of reconciliation that will transform society (see 2 Corinthians 5:18–20).

Personal Transformation

Before revival can transform society, it must first transform God's people. The apostle Paul tells us, "The god of this age has blinded the minds of unbelievers, so that they cannot see the light of the gospel of the glory of Christ, who is the image of God" (2 Corinthians 4:4). Satan has blinded the eyes of unbelievers to the truth of Christ. As Paul explains, "A veil covers their hearts" (2 Corinthians 3:15).

When God's glory releases His manifest presence, unbelievers encounter God, and the truth of the Gospel is revealed to them. God made a prophetic promise to all who would accept Christ Jesus as their Lord and Savior: "I will give you a new heart and put a new spirit in you; I will remove from you your heart of stone and give you a heart of flesh" (Ezekiel 36:26). When unbelievers receive the gift of salvation through Christ, God gives them the Holy Spirit and a new heart. The scales fall from their eyes, and they are able to see and understand spiritual realities that previously made no sense.

Many who accept Christ experience dramatic transformations from darkness into light. This is what happened to the apostle Paul, as recorded in Acts 9. Paul, known then as Saul, was an avid persecutor of Christians, but on the road to Damascus, he saw a light from heaven and heard the voice of Jesus. The experience left him blind until he received prayer from Ananias. Acts 9:18 tells us that when Ananias placed his hands on Paul and prayed for him to be filled with the Holy Spirit, "Immediately, something like scales fell from Saul's eyes, and he could see again." Paul was powerfully transformed in that moment. He understood what had not made sense to him before—the reality of Jesus Christ, His sacrificial death and His triumphant resurrection. Immediately, Paul began to preach the Gospel.

Radical transformations still happen today. Recently, a friend shared with me the following story from a revival he attended. A young gay man came to one of the meetings convinced it was a scam and that people were being paid to claim they had been healed. The young man sat through the meeting untouched by the teaching and the many healings that took place. At the end of the service, the leader announced he would lay hands on anyone who wanted an impartation of God's glory. Still convinced that nothing he had seen was real, the young man decided to get into line just to prove to himself the whole thing was a hoax.

The leader came by and lightly touched the brim of the young man's baseball cap. Instantly, the glory of God hit the young man, knocking him to the ground. He began sobbing uncontrollably, repenting and crying out to the Lord to save him. He returned the next night to testify about his radical conversion and transformation. Not only was he a believer now, he was no longer gay. All homosexual desires in him were gone!

We need more radical transformations like that today. We need another visitation of His glory. During the Jesus People Movement of the 1960s, two million teenagers were saved. Many of these were hippies who encountered the glory of God through His presence, power and goodness, and were instantly transformed. I long to see such mass transformations again, with thousands and even millions coming to Christ, surrendering everything in their desire to follow Him.

The Image of Christ

God's will is to transform God's people into the image of Christ, and His glory accomplishes this in us. The only way we become more like Jesus is to live by the Spirit. "Live by the Spirit, and you will not gratify the desires of the sinful nature" (Galatians 5:16). It is the Spirit who transforms us, touching us with His glory and giving us the grace to live consecrated, holy lives.

When God's glory descends in the form of the Holy Spirit, He convicts us of our sins. (This is what happened with the gay young man at the revival.) Jesus spoke of this when He told His disciples, "I tell you the truth: It is for your good that I am going away. Unless I go away, the Counselor will not come to you; but if I go, I will send him to you. When he comes, he will convict the world of guilt in regard to sin and righteousness and judgment" (John 16:7–8).

It may seem strange that someone sent to comfort us also convicts us of guilt and sin. That may sound like a lot of shame and condemnation. But this is never God's purpose in convicting us. He wants us to understand what we have done so we can be healed and set free from it, rather than shamed by it. As He gently reveals to us the truth about our spiritual condition we can turn to Him for the healing we need. This is not an automatic process. He is present and desires to heal us, but we must seek Him and surrender to His healing. We have an active part to play. Sadly, many Christians spend most of their lives ducking God's revelations to them because they are painful, and do not receive the deep inner healing that is vital to their consecration and intimacy with God. They know Him at a polite, less costly distance and spend their lives spiritually handicapped. We often don't recognize it, but our sin is oppressing us, squeezing the life out of us. As we turn to Him, however, He comforts us by removing our sin and setting us free. This is a process that happens over time, and God knows just how much to reveal to us and when to reveal it.

This process was at work in me when I went to Toronto in October 1994. On the first night, as I received prayer from the ministry leaders there, I did not physically shake or rattle as I expected might happen. Instead, God's glory came to me in a different way as I lay quietly on the floor. As I mentioned previously, the Holy Spirit convicted me that night of root issues causing damage to my marriage and my family. I had been a pastor for twenty years, and I was not looking for God to show me any roots of rejection and bitterness buried deep in my heart. In fact, I had no idea these things were even there. But because the Lord convicted me, I was able to see them, repent and forgive. Once I did, He brought healing to my relationships with my parents, my wife and my children. His glory set me free and transformed me at an even deeper level. As we submit to God's revelations to us, we experience transformation at even deeper levels. It is an ongoing process throughout our lives and, I think, for eternity.

This is why it is so important to spend time in the secret place of prayer with the Holy Spirit, beholding Jesus. The Spirit convicts us of our sins and gives us the grace to repent and live in holiness, while Christ provides the model for *how* we should live. As God progressively transforms us in this way, we move from glory to glory, deepening our intimacy with Him and becoming more like Jesus.

We can know we are becoming more like Jesus when we increase our capacity to love, because God is love. First John 4:7–8 says, "Everyone who loves has been born of God and knows God. Whoever does not love does not know God, because God is love." God's Great Commandment is that we love Him and love others as we love ourselves (see Matthew 22:37–39).

If we are faithful to live by the Spirit and by love, God will continue to transform us into the image of Christ. "We know that in all things God works for the good of those who love him, who have been called according to his purpose. For those God foreknew he also predestined to be conformed to the likeness of his Son" (Romans 8:28–29). God's glory comes to transform His children, and He will be faithful to complete this transformation in us until the day of Jesus Christ (see Philippians 1:6). This personal transformation is simply foundational. Without it, we cannot know the motives of our own heart, and we may do damage to others even in God's name. Only when we have been personally transformed will we become conduits of His glory and transform our surroundings.

Societal Transformation

When we have been personally transformed by the glory of God we can then impact cities and nations for Jesus. The Lord commands us, "Ask of me, and I will make the nations your inheritance, the ends of the earth your possession" (Psalm 2:8). As His children, we have been given nations as our inheritance. God trusts us and gives us dominion over the affairs of nations. He intends to restore the dominion originally given to us in the Garden of Eden.

The biblical basis for this dominion is seen as early as Genesis 1:28, when God tells Adam and Eve, "Be fruitful and multiply; fill the earth and subdue it; have dominion over the fish of the sea, over the birds of the air, and over every living thing that moves on the earth" (NKJV). God's desire is that through our intimate relationship with Him—a relationship that Adam and Eve experienced in the Garden—we also take dominion over the earth.

We forfeited our dominion in the Fall when we chose to follow the path offered by Satan. Godly dominion was restored to us only in the Person of Christ Jesus. Please note that God gave us *dominion*, not domination. Our dominion is a loving stewardship, following the pattern demonstrated to us by our heavenly Father God. Jesus summed up this dominion mandate to us in his final words, often referred to as the Great Commission: "Jesus came to them and said, 'All authority in heaven and on earth has been given to me. Therefore go and make disciples of all nations, baptizing them in the name of the Father and of the Son and of the Holy Spirit, and teaching them to obey everything I have commanded you'" (Matthew 28:18–20).

During the 1980s, a meeting of great spiritual significance occurred between Bill Bright, president and founder of Campus Crusade for Christ Ministries, and Loren Cunningham, director of Youth With a Mission (YWAM). YWAM is the largest youth missions organization in the world, with over ten thousand young people working in numerous ministry projects throughout the nations. These two major apostles met to share what each felt he had received as a fresh word from the Lord. The men quickly discovered that, independent of one another, each had received an identical word regarding the transformation of society. The meeting was clearly prophetic: God had revealed to both men the same seven "mountains of culture," along with a clear mandate that the church was to prevail in each of them. These mountains cover essentially every area of human endeavor: family, business, government, religion, education, media and arts and entertainment.[9]

I believe that God's will is for each of us to come into the fullness of our potential, and our destiny is to climb to the top of the mountain we are called to. In this way, we establish His Kingdom on earth and transform the society around us. The Bible says, "The LORD will make you the head, not the tail. If you pay attention to the commands of the LORD your God that I give you this day and carefully follow them, you will always be at the top, never at the bottom" (Deuteronomy 28:13). God wants each of us to reach the top of our mountain, using our influence to bring transformation to that realm of society, not for personal glory but for the glory of God.

Cities and Nations

One of the mountains of culture that Harvest Rock Church is called to climb is that of arts and entertainment. God has blessed our church with the beautiful Ambassador Auditorium, a world class concert hall in Pasadena, as our home— and through it, we have had extraordinary opportunities to preach the Gospel. We open the building to a variety of arts and entertainment groups throughout the year. For example, the renowned Los Angeles Chamber Orchestra uses our building to hold its concerts. Written into our standard contract with every group that uses our building is an agreement that allows us to preach the Good News of Jesus Christ. So before every concert or event at Ambassador Auditorium, one of our pastoral staff members welcomes the audience and gives a brief testimonial about Jesus.

Thousands of people who attend various performances at Ambassador Auditorium are exposed to the Gospel, and many talented performers are coming to know Jesus Christ as a result. When a scene from the movie *Dreamgirls* was filmed in our building, I had the opportunity to pray with and minister to the performer Beyoncé Knowles. Using our building to share the Good News of the Kingdom is just one way we are fulfilling God's call to transform our city.

His desire for His church is not only to transform our cities but also to transform our nation. When The Call D.C. was held in September 2000, the gathering of over four hundred thousand people fasted and prayed for God to end abortion as well as to bring revival to America. That year, our country experienced an unusual moment in our political history when, during the presidential election, votes in Florida were recounted. In the end, Al Gore won the nation's popular vote, but George W. Bush won the presidency. It cannot be overlooked that President Bush was effective in banning late-term abortion in America. In 2003 Congress passed the Partial-Birth Abortion Ban Act, with President Bush signing it into law.

President Bush also appointed Chief Justice John Roberts and Justice Samuel Alito to the U.S. Supreme Court, both of whom were crucial in the 5-4 ruling in April 2007 to uphold the ban on late-term abortion procedures. Before President Bush appointed Roberts as Chief Justice, something curious happened in the ministry of Lou Engle and the prayer warriors of the Justice House of Prayer in Washington, D.C. As the group prayed for an end to abortion, they kept receiving the name "John Roberts." Not knowing who Roberts was, they looked up his name online and started praying for him to be appointed to the Supreme Court. This was all before Roberts was first mentioned as a potential nominee by President Bush. These examples show us that our prayers and actions have the potential to affect the course of our nation.

Through Harvest International Ministry (HIM), our church's network of apostolic ministries, we are able to bring transformation not only to our nation but also to over thirty countries and 5,000 churches around the world. HIM has key leaders involved in planting churches, preaching the Gospel, caring for orphans and releasing the glory of God internationally. In all of these endeavors, I believe we are seeing the fulfillment of Jesus' words: "This gospel of the kingdom will be preached in the whole world as a testimony to all nations, and then the end will come" (Matthew 24:14).

Making Disciples of Nations

In the Great Commission, Jesus told His disciples to make disciples of all nations. He did not tell the disciples to make *believers* of all nations, but *disciples* of all nations. The emphasis here is not only on the *quantity* of converts but also on the *quality* of disciples. And this commission is not only to missionaries in foreign missions. We are *all* commanded to go into the world around us. Jesus reminds us we are surrounded by mission fields that are "white unto harvest" (see John 4:35).

Given our church's calling to the arts and entertainment, and our nearness to Hollywood, we are seeing major actors becoming radically saved. I will not reveal the names of the actors, to respect their privacy, but some of the top stars in Hollywood are becoming radical for Jesus. These actors cannot attend regular church services because they would be ambushed by fans or the paparazzi. Instead, they are discipled through Bible studies that they hold in their homes.

Peter faced a similar situation in his evangelism of Cornelius, a prominent Gentile. In Acts 10, Peter went to Cornelius' house in obedience to a vision from God, and the Gentiles there were saved, received the Holy Spirit and were baptized. But the local synagogue was not open to Cornelius as a Gentile believer. So Cornelius' friends and family asked Peter to stay with them for a few days to continue teaching them, and Peter agreed. He knew the need for these new believers to be discipled.

Discipleship is a process that involves much more than teaching principles of faith. It is living out the life of Christ in a way that clearly displays His glory. We are to walk in His power and authority and reflect His goodness to those we disciple. Jesus said that we are "the salt of the earth" (Matthew 5:13). He also called us "the light of the world" (Matthew 5:14). He told us, "Let your light shine before men, that they may see your good deeds and praise your Father in heaven" (Matthew 5:16).

In Luke 19:13, Jesus said, "Do business till I come" (NKJV). What is this business we must do? I believe we must experience revival and bring transformation to our world. We are to let the light within us shine forth and change the society around us. We are to make disciples of all nations by fulfilling the Great Commandment and completing the Great Commission.

God releases His glory for a purpose: to bring salvation and transformation to His people and the world, until the whole earth is filled with His glory. As believers, we must allow ourselves to be transformed by His glory and, in turn, release His glory throughout the world in which we live.

12

The Glory of God and the Transfer of Wealth

I realize this sounds fantastic, but sometimes when the glory of God manifests, gold, gold dust, and gems appear from nowhere. I know this is so, for I have seen it happen. While in Israel in May 2008, a gold nugget fell during one of our meetings, and a woman from our tour group handed it to me. My wife, Sue, frequently has gold dust form on her hands whenever she talks about Jesus. At Harvest Rock Church we have had numerous reports of church members instantaneously having their teeth filled with gold or covered by gold crowns. These supernatural occurrences have been verified by their dentists.

The sudden appearance of jewels and gems has happened in worship meetings around the world. A few years ago, my friend Bill Johnson, senior pastor of Bethel Church in Redding, California, showed me pictures of gems that fell into the yard of a humble couple who lived in Idaho. Bill flew out to meet this elderly couple and to take pictures of these gems. They were perfect 50-carat gems made up of stones that a gemologist could not recognize. Then in July 2008 Rob DeLuca, an HIM pastor in New Zealand, showed me two small gems he carries in his wallet. One of the gems appeared in his church during worship time. The worship leader heard something rattling in his guitar, shook the instrument, and saw the gem fall out. Another gem was found when a church member fell to the ground in worship and saw the jewel on the floor next to him. Rob has had both of these gems assessed and was told they were precious stones unlike any currently found on earth.

Why are gems appearing? Why is gold dust appearing? I believe these occurrences are prophetic signs, indicating that God is bringing prosperity to His people for the purpose of transforming society.

Glory and Wealth

The Hebrew word for "glory," *kabôd*, as discussed in the first chapter, is defined as "abundance, honor, glory, riches, wealth, splendor," according to *Strong's Dictionary*. Embedded in the very definition of glory is a "weighty splendor of wealth." And the Bible shows us there is a correlation between the glory of God and the appearance of wealth. Isaiah 60 begins with the declaration that the glory of God has come: "Arise, shine, for your light has come, and the glory of the LORD rises upon you. See, darkness covers the earth and thick darkness is over the peoples, but the LORD rises upon you and his glory appears over you" (Isaiah 60:1–2).

Many of the verses that follow in the same chapter refer to material wealth, riches and gold being brought to God's people:

154

You will look and be radiant, your heart will throb and swell with joy; the wealth on the seas will be brought to you, to you the riches of the nations will come. Herds of camels will cover your land, young camels of Midian and Ephah. And all from Sheba will come, bearing gold and incense and proclaiming the praise of the LORD.

Isaiah 60:5–6

This same principle of glory-followed-by-wealth is also found in Haggai:

"I will shake all the nations; and they will come with the wealth of all nations, and I will fill this house with glory," says the LORD of hosts. "The silver is Mine and the gold is Mine," declares the LORD of hosts.

Haggai 2:7–8, NASB

Haggai made this prophetic statement as the Temple was being reconstructed. So this passage carries dual ramifications. In one sense, it refers to the physical Temple of the Lord being restored and rebuilt under Ezra. In another sense, I believe the verse also speaks prophetically about another temple, a spiritual one: God's Church. The Lord will fill His Church, the Body of Christ, with glory, and the wealth of the nations will come to His people.

The Great Transfer of Wealth

Many Christians today have great difficulty believing God wants to bless them materially. This is due, in no small part, to centuries of teaching in the church that poverty produces godly humility and builds Christlike character, while wealth is viewed as an evil and corrupting influence. Certainly the love or worship of money will get you into a lot of trouble, as Scripture makes abundantly clear. But it is also possible

155

to be completely obsessed with money while not having a dime.

Exalting poverty in such a way is completely unscriptural. The Bible states repeatedly that God wants His people to prosper. Jeremiah 29:11 says, "'I know the plans I have for you,' declares the LORD, 'plans to prosper you and not to harm you, plans to give you hope and a future.'" Likewise, Deuteronomy 28:11 says, "The LORD will grant you abundant prosperity—in the fruit of your womb, the young of your livestock and the crops of your ground—in the land he swore to your forefathers to give you." God desires to bless His people *materially and abundantly*.

His blessings include wealth, as indicated in Proverbs 10:22: "The blessing of the LORD brings wealth, and he adds no trouble to it." Wealth comes from the Lord (see 1 Chronicles 29:12), and when we are under God's Lordship, He desires to prosper us. David observed, "I was young and now I am old, yet I have never seen the righteous forsaken or their children begging bread. They are always generous and lend freely; their children will be blessed" (Psalm 37:25–26). God blesses His righteous ones so abundantly they are able to lend money and have enough for their own children as well.

Scripture also makes clear that God wants to transfer the wealth of the unrighteous to the righteous: "A good man leaves an inheritance for his children's children, but a sinner's wealth is stored up for the righteous" (Proverbs 13:22). The Bible is filled with examples of wealth being transferred to God's people.

In Exodus, Moses instructed the Israelites to ask for wealth from the Egyptians before leaving.

The Israelites did as Moses instructed and asked the Egyptians for articles of silver and gold and for clothing. The LORD had made the Egyptians favorably disposed toward the people, and they gave them what they asked for; so they plundered the Egyptians.

Exodus 12:35–36

The wealth of the Egyptians was transferred to the Israelites as God delivered His people from slavery. Another example of the transfer of wealth is found in Ezra:

In the first year of King Cyrus, the king issued a decree concerning the temple of God in Jerusalem: Let the temple be rebuilt as a place to present sacrifices, and let its foundations be laid. It is to be ninety feet high and ninety feet wide, with three courses of large stones and one of timbers. The costs are to be paid by the royal treasury. Also, the gold and silver articles of the house of God, which Nebuchadnezzar took from the temple in Jerusalem and brought to Babylon, are to be returned to their places in the temple in Jerusalem; they are to be deposited in the house of God.

Ezra 6:3–5

The Persian King Cyrus declared he would rebuild the Temple of God in Jerusalem, paid for from the royal treasury of Persia. Moreover, Cyrus commanded the restoration of all the silver and gold that Nebuchadnezzar had taken from the Temple. He even declared that the Jews who worked on the Temple would be paid out of the royal treasury and that he would provide without fail whatever materials the priests needed (Ezra 6:8–10).

It was God who moved Cyrus to make this decree. So the wealth of the Persians was transferred to God's people, all for the purpose of rebuilding His Temple.

The Transfer Today

Today, God still desires prosperity for His people. The promises of the Bible have not changed. Deuteronomy 8:18 says,

"Remember the LORD your God, for it is he who gives you the ability to produce wealth, and so confirms his covenant, which he swore to your forefathers, as it is today." The Jews are still God's chosen people, and God has continued to prosper them, just as He promised Abraham in Genesis 12 and 13. But through our relationship with Jesus Christ, all believers are now able to receive the riches of the Abrahamic covenant as their inheritance.

God continues to transfer wealth to His people today. We are starting to see some of these transfers take place.

- In 1997, Pat Robertson sold The Family Channel, a satellite-delivered cable-television network owned by the Christian Broadcasting Network, to Fox Kids Worldwide, Inc. The sale price was $1.9 billion. The channel was later acquired by Disney and changed to ABC Family in 2001.[1]
- In 2004, Joan B. Kroc, widow of the founder of Mc-Donald's Corporation, donated $1.5 billion to the Salvation Army, a Christian organization. According to the Associated Press, "Kroc's gift is the largest ever to a charitable organization and ranks ninth overall in terms of gifts to nonprofit organizations."[2]
- In early 2006, Dan L. Duncan, chairman of the energy services company, Enterprise Products Partners, donated $100 million to Baylor University's College of Medicine to fund a new cancer center.[3] Baylor University is a Southern Baptist organization. The transfer of wealth is happening among evangelicals, and I rejoice with them.

Transfers of wealth are also taking place internationally for apostolic charismatic churches. I know a pastor in Indonesia, Alex Tanuseputra, who oversees an apostolic network of eight hundred churches throughout Southeast Asia and whose own church is one of the largest in Indonesia, with over eighty thousand members. God spoke to Alex to build a prayer tower that would be the tallest building in the world. Alex believes the proposed structure, Jakarta Tower, will be a prophetic sign that Christians are to be the head and not the tail (see Deuteronomy 28:13). In an interview with *United World*, Alex stated, "Above all, the main aim of the tower is to give back to the community, providing jobs and operating quality programs such as educational and religious for two hundred million people. The Lord has helped us by providing us with investors and donations."[4]

God has miraculously provided the wealth to fund this extravagant building project, which is scheduled for completion in 2010. One surprising source came through a businessman in Alex's church. This man had ignored a coalmine he owned and focused on his other ventures when the price of coal plummeted due to China's policy of open coal production. Eventually, the mines in China caused significant environmental problems and the government had to close them. At that point, the businessman reopened his coalmine to produce what he thought was three hundred million tons of coal. To his surprise, he found the mine contained over one billion tons of coal. Moreover, when the mines reopened to dig for coal, oil was discovered as well. The Christian businessman's first tithe from his profit was $45 million, and it went to fund Jakarta Tower.

I believe our church building in Pasadena, the Ambassador Auditorium, is also a prophetic sign of the great transfer of wealth. The building was constructed and owned by Herbert Armstrong and the Worldwide Church of God. This sect was identified as a heretical cult because of its non-biblical doctrines and criticisms of traditional Christianity.[5] Eventually the Worldwide Church of God rejected those non-biblical doctrines and became a member of the National Association of Evangelicals. After this, they offered to sell their beautiful Ambassador Auditorium to our church. God miraculously provided the finances for Harvest Rock to buy the building.

The Ambassador Auditorium sits at the "head" of our city, in the location where the annual Tournament of Roses Parade begins. The auditorium's ceiling is covered with 24-karat pure gold leaf. A $1 million chandelier decorates the entrance. The wall is made of pure onyx, a gemstone. I believe our use of the building to advance God's Kingdom and transform our society speaks prophetically of His great transfer of wealth.

We are never to limit the Holy One of Israel. Isaiah 60:11 tells us, "Your gates will always stand open, they will never be shut, day or night, so that men may bring you the wealth of the nations—their kings led in triumphal procession." Day and night, the Lord will continue to prosper His children, transferring wealth from the ungodly to the righteous.

Principles for Prosperity

God wants to prosper His people. Yet we will only be entrusted with wealth if we steward God's blessings faithfully and properly. The Bible says, "The earth is the LORD's, and everything in it, the world, and all who live in it" (Psalm 24:1). Everything in heaven and earth belongs to God, the Creator (see 1 Chronicles 29:11), and we must have His wisdom and understanding to act as stewards of His creation. The following are six important principles for prosperity:

1. Stewardship

Wealth and honor come from our Father, the ruler of all things (1 Chronicles 29:12). When we receive wealth from God, we are to see ourselves as stewards, rather than owners. What is stewardship? To understand it, we may examine the function of a financial planner as a model of stewardship.

Financial planners do not own the money they have been assigned to manage. Their job involves looking for investment opportunities to generate larger financial returns for the owners of the accounts they oversee.

Similarly, as God's children, we must properly steward what God has given us, including His gifts, talents and finances. These all belong to God anyway. Jesus says those who are not faithful with little will not be given the opportunity to be faithful with much (see Luke 16:10). But if we are faithful with what God has already given us, He will gladly give us more. David sings of God's faithfulness in 2 Samuel 22:26, "To the faithful you show yourself faithful."

2. Obedience

In addition to understanding the principle of stewardship, we need to walk in obedience to God. He will not trust His wealth to anyone who does not walk in obedience and submit himself to Christ's Lordship. The Bible says, "The LORD commanded us to obey all these decrees and to fear the LORD our God, so that we might always prosper and be kept alive, as is the case today" (Deuteronomy 6:24). The blessings of prosperity come with a condition: We must first obey what the Lord commands. And Scripture says if we obey and revere the Lord, we will prosper in all we do (see Deuteronomy 29:9).

3. Character

We must also grow in character and wholeness, so God can trust us with His blessings and wealth. Money can be a tremendous blessing if it is seen as a means to bless others. But if money is seen as an end and not as a means, it can corrupt us. The Bible says, "For the love of money is a root of all kinds of evil. Some people, eager for money, have wandered from the faith and pierced themselves with many griefs" (1 Timothy 6:10). The *love* of money is the root of all evil, not the money itself. Without the necessary character in our attitude toward money, we cannot expect God to transfer wealth to us.

4. Repentance

Another important consideration in the transfer of wealth involves repenting of a "poverty mentality." This spirit of poverty entered the church during the third century, leading to the development of institutional Christian monasticism, which required a vow of poverty. Over time poverty became equated with piety. I have no objections to Christians wanting to live simply, but legislating poverty for everyone else is an act of legalism. The spirit of poverty is still very much in our churches today. And it is important to repent of a poverty mentality: "Repent, for the kingdom of heaven is near" (Matthew 4:17). Repenting of a poverty mentality will allow us to change our thinking and activate our faith, enabling us to receive the blessings of prosperity God desires to give us.

5. Sowing

Giving back to God in the form of tithes and offerings is another important factor in receiving the transfer of wealth. The Lord blesses those who give back to Him. When people vacillate over whether to tithe or struggle with giving money back to God, it is a sign to me they have not surrendered everything to Jesus as Lord.

When I was saved, I was told I had to give 10 percent of my income to the Lord. I agreed immediately because I knew this was a command in the Bible (see Genesis 14:18–20; Leviticus 27:30–33; Malachi 3:6–12; Matthew 23:23). I didn't need to reflect and mull it over. Scripture said it and that settled it for me. Paul tells us, "Whoever sows sparingly will also reap sparingly, and whoever sows generously will also reap generously. Each man should give what he has decided in his heart to give, not reluctantly or under compulsion, for God loves a cheerful giver" (2 Corinthians 9:6–7). Those who faithfully give back to God will be given more.

6. Prosperity with a Purpose

Finally, we must understand that God prospers His people for a purpose. By His grace and through His glory, He equips us to advance His Kingdom, to transform society and to be salt and light in the world. And He entrusts us with wealth in order to bring His Kingdom to earth through the transformation of culture. This may sound like "mission impossible," something that can happen only after Christ returns. But we must remember it was Christ who taught us to pray for His kingdom to come and for His will to be done on earth as it is in heaven. I believe that He meant for this prayer to be fulfilled, and He gave us a mandate to work for that fulfillment.

Let me give you an outstanding example of how God is using the transfer of wealth to advance His Kingdom. A few years ago on a trip to China, I was privileged to meet a "marketplace apostle"—that is, someone who is doing apostolic work outside the walls of the church. (I need to withhold the man's name for security reasons.) He is an American business-man who felt a missionary call to China in his early twenties when he was still a university student. After he graduated, he went to China to teach English for two years. When he completed that commitment, he wanted to stay in China as a missionary, but it was impossible to obtain a visa for missionary work. So he applied for a business visa instead. Although his first choice was to be a missionary, not a businessman, opportunities presented themselves and he was able to start several profitable businesses.

That was almost thirty years ago. Today, this man is one of the most successful businessmen in China. He owns over ten companies and is a millionaire many times over. In operating his companies, he continues to use the skills he learned as a teacher of English, when he first came to China—only now he employs these skills to advance the Gospel. For example, he offers free English lessons to all his executives and employees who want to learn the language—and he uses the Bible as a textbook! Many of his employees have come to know the Lord through this unique workplace evangelism.

As a result of his success in business, he teamed up with another successful Christian businessman to build one of the most prestigious universities in China. The two men hired top professors with doctorates from western universities such as Oxford, Cambridge and the Ivy League schools, offering top wages to attract them. And they made sure all the professors they hired were Christians!

God gave the two businessmen tremendous favor with Chinese government officials. Their status as successful entrepreneurs provided them access to the core members of the Politburo. They strategically "wined and dined" each core member and persuaded every one to agree that the professors could teach their various subjects in a context with Christian values. The Chinese officials actually welcomed this. In recent years, they have discovered that Christian values of integrity and honor toward parents, as well as submitting to governing authorities, is in line with China's national values.

The only prohibition placed on the professors is they are not allowed to preach the Gospel during the day in the classroom. During the evenings, however, they are free to hold Bible studies and Christian services. Because of the university's impressive teaching staff and excellent curriculum, the government is sending their top students there. These students will be the future government leaders of China, as well as the CEOs of China's corporations. At this writing, fifteen thousand students are enrolled, and already more than three thousand have accepted Jesus. These students are not only converts, but also disciples in training to transform the culture in China.

The businessman who had wanted to be a missionary knew that God gave him such abundant prosperity for a purpose. Indeed, the amazing university he co-founded could never have existed if it were not for the missionary zeal of two businessmen who gave literally hundreds of millions of dollars to build it. Though this man originally wanted to be a traditional missionary in the field, God had a larger purpose in view and a much larger missionary field in mind. Now a harvest is being yielded that promises to transform a nation.

As this example so powerfully illustrates, God's purpose in transferring wealth to His people is to transform entire societies. When money is used for this purpose, God is glorified, and His Kingdom is advanced in powerful ways, often beyond our imagination!

13

The Glory of God in the Last Days

Over the years as a pastor, I have heard repeated concerns regarding the last days leading up to the Second Coming of Jesus Christ. Various people have developed different theories on the end times. For example, a number of Christian leaders have issued warnings that recent earthquakes and floods are sent by the Lord as a form of judgment to individual nations. Some believers predict times of tremendous persecution against the Church. Others express the need to stay protected and hidden among other Christians in "cities of refuge."

The Last Days

My desire in this chapter is to express what the Bible says about the last days. I have identified five principles set forth in Scripture regarding the glory of God in the last days.

1. The Latter House and the Former House

The first principle of the glory of God in the last days is: *The latter house will be more glorious than the former house.*

This principle is taken directly from Haggai:

> "I will shake all the nations; and they will come with the wealth of all nations, and I will fill this house with glory," says the LORD of hosts. "The silver is Mine and the gold is Mine," declares the LORD of hosts. "The latter glory of this house will be greater than the former," says the LORD of hosts, "and in this place I will give peace," declares the LORD of hosts.
>
> Haggai 2:7–9, NASB

What does the Lord mean when He tells us the latter house will be greater than the former house? This simply means that the *latter glory* will be greater than the *former glory*. Let me explain.

If we take the literal-grammatical-historical interpretation of Haggai, he was prophesying that the Temple built under Zerubbabel would be more glorious that the Temple built under King Solomon. However, a prophecy can have multiple applications. I also believe Haggai was prophesying into the period we live in now. This period began after Jesus died on the cross, rose again, ascended into heaven and poured out His Spirit. There is no doubt that this period—under the New Covenant, involving the past two thousand years—has been more glorious than the former period, which was under the Law or the Old Covenant (see Hebrews 7:22; 8:6).

Jesus spoke of this greater glory when He said to His disciples, "I tell you the truth, anyone who has faith in me will do what I have been doing. He will do even greater things than these, because I am going to the Father" (John 14:12). Christ is saying that we have access to greater glory through

His death and resurrection. And according to His own testimony, we are able to perform greater works and miracles than even He did when He was on earth. I sometimes hear Christians say, "I wish I lived in the days of the New Testament." I believe the apostles and prophets of the early New Testament times longed to experience what we are entering into in these last days before Christ returns!

Paul talks about the increasing latter glory in 2 Corinthians 3:18: "But we all, with unveiled face, beholding as in a mirror the glory of the Lord, are being transformed into the same image from glory to glory, just as by the Spirit of the Lord" (NKJV). I have mentioned that even though Moses experienced the glory of God, it was a fading glory. Under the New Covenant we have received through Jesus, we have access to a glory that is ever increasing, as we are continually transformed into the likeness of our Lord. And we can be confident we will continue to experience an increase in glory until Jesus Christ returns.

2. Hosting the Spirit of Revival

The second principle regarding God's glory in the last days is: *God's glory will dwell in a house where the Spirit of revival is invited.*

We know the glory of God dwells within us when we accept Jesus into our hearts. The Bible says Christ in us is the hope of glory (see Colossians 1:27), and our bodies are to be a temple of the Holy Spirit. Therefore, some Christians say, "God is everywhere and He is in me. I don't have to go anyplace for revival. I can have it right here and now." This is partially true. But the glory of God, meaning His manifest presence, has historically descended upon specific locations in times of revival. The Spirit fell on Azusa Street in 1906. He manifested in Toronto in 1994. So why does the Holy Spirit visit certain localities and churches?

The fact is God honors those who persistently hunger and thirst for Him. His glory will be found wherever His presence is sought and welcomed. David expresses this when he sings in Psalm 26:8, "I love the house where you live, O LORD, the place where your glory dwells." And Psalm 96:6 echoes, "Splendor and majesty are before him; strength and glory are in his sanctuary."

I believe we can learn how to host the Holy Spirit in our homes, in our small groups and in our churches. When we persistently seek the presence of God, He will build in our gatherings a habitation in which His glory dwells. "For where two or three come together in my name, there am I with them" (Matthew 18:20). When we as believers gather together, Jesus says He will be with us, and we become carriers of His glory.

3. Glory and Darkness

The third principle regarding God's glory in the last days is: *There will be both glory and darkness in the last days.* The Bible tells us this in Isaiah:

"Arise, shine, for your light has come, and the glory of the LORD rises upon you. See, darkness covers the earth and thick darkness is over the peoples, but the LORD rises upon you and His glory appears over you. Nations will come to your light, and kings to the brightness of your dawn."

Isaiah 60:1–3

Isaiah prophesies that light and darkness will coexist on the earth, but that the darkness covering the earth will be invaded by God's glory.

There is darkness in the world today. It is evident in the illegal financial ethics too often displayed in our workplaces. Darkness infiltrates the philosophy of humanism taught in many of our universities. It dwells in the violence, drug abuse and deep despair that have become all too common in our communities.

We are commanded to bring the light of God's glory to a world stumbling in darkness. We hear it frequently said, "There are many paths to truth," but not all roads lead us out of darkness and into the light. Jesus says in John 14:6, "I am the way and the truth and the life. No one comes to the Father except through me." Christ is the *only* way, and those who do not know Him are living and walking in darkness.

In Pakistan, our HIM apostle (whose name I withhold for security reasons) says the greatest harvest he's currently seeing is among Al Qaeda radical terrorists. As they encounter the glory of God through His people, they are coming out of the darkness of jihad terrorism and into the light of Christ. Jesus prophesied, "You are the light of the world" (Matthew 5:14). As carriers of His glory, we shine His light wherever there is darkness.

God wants us to "declare his glory among all nations, his marvelous deeds among all peoples" (Psalm 96:3). We can change the darkness into light with His glory. Isaiah 60:2 tells us, "The LORD rises upon you and his glory appears over you." Even the smallest amount of light is greater than the deepest darkness. A person in a pitch-black cave can light a tiny match and see the darkness disappear. Jesus commands, "Let your light shine before men, that they may see your good deeds and praise your Father in heaven" (Matthew 5:16).

The book of Acts contains a wonderful story about how two apostles in a very dark situation brought light to one of their captors. While imprisoned, Paul and Silas were praying and singing hymns to God when a violent earthquake shook the jail. Suddenly all the prison doors flew open and every prisoner's chains came undone. Seeing the glory of God displayed in their miraculous deliverance, the Philippian jailer asked, "Sirs, what must I do to be saved?" (Acts 16:30). Paul and Silas replied,

"Believe in the Lord Jesus, and you will be saved—you and your household" (16:31). The jailer and his entire household came to the light: "He was filled with joy because he had come to believe in God—he and his whole family" (16:34). God wants us to bring His glory outside the four walls of the church and into the world, where there is darkness. He wants entire households to be saved, just like the Philippian jailer's.

If we will carry His light to others, the Lord will manifest His glory. I once attended a revival where every morning session was dedicated to teaching its attendees how to minister God's glory to the world through signs, wonders and evangelism. The attendees were encouraged to go into the city every afternoon and ask the Holy Spirit to lead them to "glory opportunities." One group of attendees went to a restaurant for lunch where they saw a family with a need. The mother was in a wheelchair and was accompanied by her husband and children. The group learned this mother had fractured her spine and was living in great pain daily. She agreed to let the group pray for her, and when they did, she was instantly and miraculously healed. She and her whole family prayed to receive the Lord on the spot. They were so excited that they changed their plans for that evening and came to the revival instead. They wanted to give God glory, and they were only two hours old in the faith!

Jesus commanded His disciples, "Heal the sick, raise the dead, cleanse those who have leprosy, drive out demons. Freely you have received, freely give" (Matthew 10:8). God wants us to show His love to those around us who are living in darkness. He wants us to let our light shine before men. As we do what Jesus commanded, we will see God's glory invade the darkness.

4. A Glory-Filled Earth

The fourth principle regarding God's glory in the last days is: *The whole earth will be filled with the glory of the Lord.*

A number of verses in the Bible prophetically declare this principle:

> Be exalted, O God, above the heavens; let your glory be over all the earth.
>
> Psalm 57:5

> Praise be to his glorious name forever; may the whole earth be filled with his glory. Amen and Amen.
>
> Psalm 72:19

> And they were calling to one another: "Holy, holy, holy is the LORD Almighty; the whole earth is full of his glory."
>
> Isaiah 6:3

> Nevertheless, as surely as I live and as surely as the glory of the LORD fills the whole earth.
>
> Numbers 14:21

> For the earth will be filled with the knowledge of the glory of the LORD, as the waters cover the sea.
>
> Habakkuk 2:14

The Bible is very clear: In the end, we win, because of Jesus. In the book of Revelation, John hears loud voices in heaven declaring, "The kingdom of the world has become the kingdom of our Lord and of his Christ, and he will reign for ever and ever" (Revelation 11:15).

The glory of the Lord will fill the earth, but I do not believe we have to wait until Jesus Christ comes in the Millennium for this to happen. I see Scripture teaching that we can see its fulfillment now. Jesus asked, "When the Son of Man comes, will he find faith on the earth?" (Luke 18:8). I want to believe God, and I will not limit the Holy One of Israel. The Lord says, "I will pour out my Spirit on all people" (Joel 2:28; Acts 2:17). I am claiming this prophetic promise from Him.

Jesus Himself said, "This gospel of the kingdom will be preached in the whole world as a testimony to all nations [all people groups], and then the end will come" (Matthew 24:14). My understanding of the last days (eschatology) is based on this passage as well as the passage in Romans 11:26, that "all Israel will be saved." We must preach the Gospel, the Good News with signs and wonders following, to all nations, *and then* the end will come. We cannot just project the coming of God's glory to a future time in the Millennium. We need His glory *now*! We have our job to do, which is to carry God's glory to the nations, to every people group.

Habakkuk prophesies, "The earth will be filled with the knowledge of the glory of the LORD" (Habakkuk 2:14). This passage does not say that everyone will be saved, but that the earth will be filled with the *knowledge* of God's glory. People will know about Jesus and witness His glory.

Right now, there are over 3.5 billion people who have not heard the Gospel. God's glory is meant for the harvest of souls. And for that reason we are to share the Gospel of Jesus Christ through signs, wonders and evangelism based on demonstrations of His power and glory.

5. The Second Coming

The fifth and last principle regarding God's glory in the last days is: *The fullness of God's glory will come at the Second Coming of Jesus.*

When Jesus returns He will come in His full glory:

> "At that time the sign of the Son of Man will appear in the sky, and all the nations of the earth will mourn. They will see the Son of Man coming on the clouds of the sky, with power and great glory."

> Matthew 24:30

"When the Son of Man comes in his glory, and all the angels with him, he will sit on his throne in heavenly glory."

Matthew 25:31

"At that time men will see the Son of Man coming in clouds with great power and glory."

Mark 13:26

With the fullness of Jesus' glory will also come judgment. "The Son of Man is going to come in his Father's glory with his angels, and then he will reward each person according to what he has done" (Matthew 16:27).

There will be two judgments in the last days:

- Everyone who is not saved will be judged at the *Great White Throne of Judgment*. "All the nations will be gathered before him, and he will separate the people one from another as a shepherd separates the sheep from the goats. He will put the sheep on his right and the goats on his left" (Matthew 25:32–33). On the Day of Judgment, those who have received salvation through Jesus will have access to heaven and all others will not.

- All born-again believers in Jesus will be judged at the *Judgment Seat of Christ*. "For we must all appear before the judgment seat of Christ, that each one may receive what is due him for the things done while in the body, whether good or bad" (2 Corinthians 5:10). As Christians, we all will go to heaven. But we will be rewarded differently, according to how we have stewarded our time, money, gifts and resources.

Are Disasters Judgment from God?

I believe in these two judgments—the Great White Throne of Judgment and the Judgment Seat of Christ—as they are clearly stated in the Bible. But I disagree with the idea that God sends earthquakes, tsunamis or other natural disasters in wrath as forms of judgment.

Ever since the Fall of man, the earth has been groaning. "We know that the whole creation has been groaning as in the pains of childbirth right up to the present time" (Romans 8:22). When humanity fell, nature did too. Sin destroyed the harmony in nature that God created, and ever since then there have been hurricanes, earthquakes, tsunamis and floods.

I do not believe God sent the earthquake to the Sichuan province of China in 2008 to judge the Chinese people. Innocent lives, including babies, were killed. Similarly, I do not believe God sent Hurricane Katrina or brought the terrorist attack on the Twin Towers as judgment on the United States. Churches were flooded by Katrina. Christians were killed in the Twin Towers. Yes, there will be judgment by God, but we know when His judgment will take place: The wicked will be judged at the Great White Throne on the Day of Judgment. And Christians will be judged at the Judgment Seat of Christ, where they will be rewarded according to their lives on earth, with all believers given access to heaven.

To know God's attitude toward natural calamities, I believe we can look at the life of Jesus. There was not one storm He liked. Whenever Jesus faced a storm, He rebuked it. "He got up and rebuked the wind and the raging waters; the storm subsided, and all was calm" (Luke 8:24). Jesus never sent a storm to attack a city that did not receive Him or obey His commands. In fact, He rebuked His disciples when they wanted Him to do this. When the Samaritans opposed Jesus, James and John wanted to call fire down from heaven to destroy them. But Jesus told them, "You do not know what kind of spirit you are of" (Luke 9:55, NASB).

The Lord's desire is that none would perish (see 2 Peter 3:9). He does not take pleasure in the death of anyone (see Ezekiel 18:32). And I believe we are to stand in the gap and pray against storms, just as Jesus demonstrated. I remember when Pat Robertson prayed on television to rebuke a powerful hurricane that was coming up the Atlantic coast toward the Virginia Beach area. At the last minute, that hurricane spun off and went in a different direction.

God does not need to add extra punishment to sin. Sin carries in itself its own judgment. The Bible tells us, "For the wages of sin is death" (Romans 6:23). Sin leads to death, oppression and sickness. If we sow sin, we reap the consequences. But Jesus came to give us life. He said, "I have come that they may have life, and have it to the full" (John 10:10).

Jesus came into the world to save it, not to condemn it (see John 3:17). When He returns, He will come in the fullness of His glory, and that glory will fill the earth. But until then, we can experience His glory in increasing measure and bring His glory into the world—glory that will transform lives and disciple nations.

14

Giving God All the Glory

In this book, we have explored God's glory as His manifest presence, which demonstrates both His goodness and His power. We have uncovered how to receive His glory, how to go from glory to glory, and how to steward His glory properly. Now there is one final aspect of glory we have yet to mention, and I want to address it in this final chapter.

The glory of God reveals His eternal majesty and calls people to recognize Him, reflect Him and glorify Him. When God reveals His glory to us, it comes with an inherent responsibility on our part. That responsibility is to give glory back to God. This is the final aspect of glory: that we are to give God glory through our praise and worship of Him.

The Bible tells us, "So whether you eat or drink or whatever you do, do it all for the glory of God" (1 Corinthians 10:31). This has been one of the key verses in my life and ministry. As God's renewed creation, we are called to glorify Him through our praise and worship, our thoughts and actions and the whole of our lives. Everything we do we should do to glorify God, who is worthy of all praise.

The Psalms often speak of giving God the praise due Him:

Sing the glory of his name; make his praise glorious!

Psalm 66:2

All the nations you have made will come and worship before you, O Lord; they will bring glory to your name.

Psalm 86:9

Ascribe to the LORD the glory due his name; bring an offering and come into his courts.

Psalm 96:8

All glory belongs to God, and He will not share this type of glory with others. The Lord declares, "I am the LORD; that is my name! I will not give my glory to another or my praise to idols" (Isaiah 42:8). He commands us not to worship idols, which may sound strangely out of place to us today. We don't have idols or shrines set up in our homes—or do we? An idol is anything or anyone we give our primary focus to rather than God. It could be our career, our home or possessions, our favorite TV programs or websites, even our spouse or children. Anything that competes with God for our time, attention, resources or affections is an idol. All of our worship and praise belong to the Lord.

Just as all glory belongs to God, we are not to take His glory upon ourselves. Instead, we are to have the attitude expressed in Psalm 115:1: "Not to us, O LORD, not to us but to your name be the glory, because of your love and faithfulness." God alone is worthy of His creation's praise, and we are called to give Him glory for who He is: our Father, Creator, Deliverer, Savior and King.

In addition to worshiping God for who He is, we should also praise Him for what He has done. Because of the Lord's great faithfulness (see Lamentations 3:23), we have countless reasons for which to give Him thanks. I want to focus on seven particular areas that God has impressed upon my heart.

Give God Glory for Life

We are to praise God for giving us *life*. Revelation 4:11 says, "You are worthy, our Lord and God, to receive glory and honor and power, for you created all things, and by your will they were created and have their being."

God is the Maker and Creator of us all. It is only by His will that each of us exists, lives and breathes here on earth. Every moment of our lives was created by God and given to us as a gift. Each of us is wonderfully created, formed and fashioned by His hand. David had a revelation of this truth: "For you created my inmost being; you knit me together in my mother's womb. I praise you because I am fearfully and wonderfully made; your works are wonderful, I know that full well" (Psalm 139:13–14).

We are all here on earth because of God's will. Before the foundations of the world were established, God knew you, envisioned you and planned for you to come into being. David continues in Psalm 139:15–16, "My frame was not hidden from you when I was made in the secret place. When I was woven together in the depths of the earth, your eyes saw my unformed body. All the days ordained for me were written in your book before one of them came to be."

Even before we were born, the Lord planned a specific destiny for each of us. And He gave us life on earth so we could fulfill His purpose for us. We are also created in God's image (see Genesis 1:26). The Bible tells us, "You have made him a little lower than God, and You crown him with glory and majesty" (Psalm 8:5, NASB). God made us a little lower than Himself. And we are seated with Jesus Christ in the heavenly places (see Ephesians 2:6). God has given us incredible authority and honor. In response, we need to give God glory for our lives.

Give God Glory for Salvation

I thank God He delivered me from the dominion of darkness and transferred me into the Kingdom of His beloved Son. It is through Christ Jesus that we have eternal life. He bought and paid for each of our lives through His death on the cross. "To the only God our Savior be glory, majesty, power and authority, through Jesus Christ our Lord, before all ages, now and forevermore! Amen" (Jude 25). We each have infinite worth in God's eyes, and He has paid for each of us with the blood of His Son.

When I think about my life before I received Jesus, I realize that I might now be dead or doing time in prison, had He not changed my lifestyle. I was once a drug addict who lived in rebellion. But because of His love, mercy and grace, God saved me and transformed me. Truly, it is by God's grace that I am who I am today, in His service (see 1 Corinthians 15:10). I thank the Lord for rescuing me and for being my Savior.

We can also be thankful that God is not only saving us but also sanctifying us. Paul writes, "And this is my prayer: that your love may abound more and more in knowledge and depth of insight, so that you may be able to discern what is best and may be pure and blameless until the day of Christ, filled with the fruit of righteousness that comes through Jesus Christ—to the glory and praise of God" (Philippians 1:9–11). Paul gives God praise for the fruit of righteousness in our lives. Likewise, we are to be thankful to God for blessing us with His Spirit to help us become holy and righteous. He has blessed us with His gift of salvation and with the Holy Spirit who lives within us.

Give God Glory for Family

The Bible says, "He who finds a wife finds what is good and receives favor from the LORD" (Proverbs 18:22). This also holds true for a woman who finds a husband. We are to thank God for our spouses.

We also need to thank God for our parents. Godly parents are a blessing from the Lord. My mother and grandmother prayed me into the Kingdom of God.

And we are to thank God for our children. *The Message* says in Psalm 127:3, "Don't you see that children are GOD's best gift? the fruit of the womb his generous legacy?" I believe that, apart from salvation, the best gift we can receive from God is children.

The moment my wife, Sue, became pregnant with each of our children, we started praying for them. We prayed specifically for three things: that they would come to know Jesus at a young age, that they would marry the person God wanted for them and that they would fulfill their destinies in Him. All of our prayers are being answered, and it is amazing to see the fruit of the prayers we have sown for our children. Your children may be in rebellion, but you can thank God now for them as you contend for their salvation.

Because of my four children, I can say to God, "I am a rich man." To have children who love Jesus Christ is a godly legacy and a truly amazing blessing from God.

Give God Glory for Favor and Blessings

God is a good God who pours out His favor and blessings on His people. Psalm 118:26 tells us, "Blessed is he who comes in the name of the LORD. From the house of the LORD we will bless you."

One Sunday morning last year, I asked my church congregation, "How many of you have had major promotions at work, or have witnessed God's favor and blessings in a major way in the last two years?" I could scarcely believe the overwhelming number of hands that went up. God wants to bless His children, and when He does, it is important that we give Him glory and praise.

Years ago, someone said that we all need to be "Teflon Christians." In other words, we need to let all glory slip off of us and go right back to God. We cannot let the praises of man stick to us, but rather, we should give God all the glory for His favor, blessings and open doors in our lives.

I have learned to thank God immediately when He gives me favor and open doors. And when people encourage me, I have learned to be gracious by saying, "Thank you." Many Christians feel compelled to respond to encouragement by saying, "Oh, it wasn't me, it was all the Lord." But I feel it is important to thank people for their encouragement. After I receive their words, I build an altar before the Lord in my heart and say, "God, I give you all the praise and all the glory."

Give God Glory for Your Work and Ministry

Paul says, "Therefore I glory in Christ Jesus in my service to God" (Romans 15:17). We are to give God glory through our service in ministry to Him.

The Bible says, "(He) has made us kings and priests to His God and Father, to Him be glory and dominion forever and ever. Amen" (Revelation 1:6, NKJV). God has made us both kings and priests. Do you know you are a king and a priest? A king is a person with dominion and authority, and a priest is a minister. In our church we teach that everyone is a minister.

If you are in the marketplace, that is your ministry. Only 1 percent of the church is in vocational, full-time ministry, and the other 99 percent are in the marketplace. We need to recognize that we each have a divine destiny and assignment, and we need to be prepared to work toward the harvest of souls, wherever God places us.

If you sometimes wonder, "How can I possibly minister to other people?" you are not alone. Moses had serious doubts about his ability to do what the Lord instructed. God had to rebuke Moses for saying he could not speak well enough and couldn't lead the Israelites. The Lord said to Moses, "Who gave man his mouth? Who makes him deaf or mute? Who gives him sight or makes him blind? Is it not I, the LORD? Now go; I will help you speak and will teach you what to say" (Exodus 4:11–12). It is the Lord who speaks through us. He will give each of us the grace to fulfill our destiny when we position ourselves according to His will.

Jesus said to His Father, "I have brought you glory on earth by completing the work you gave me to do" (John 17:4). Likewise, I want to finish the race well and strong (see 2 Timothy 4:7) by fulfilling my divine assignment here on earth. At the Judgment Seat of Christ, the Lord will hand out rewards, according to what we have accomplished with our lives (see 2 Corinthians 5:10). Whatever your job or ministry is, do it well for His glory.

Give God Glory for Revival

We receive an indwelling of the glory of God when we receive Jesus Christ into our hearts. But the glory that comes when God pours out His manifest presence is called *revival*. Just as we need to thank God for our salvation, we need to also thank God for revival.

I have been a Christian since March of 1973, when I was part of the Jesus People Movement. When I saw the revival with John Wimber in the 1980s, I did not jump in as I should have. But when the Spirit fell in Toronto in 1994, I jumped in immediately because I was desperate for God. With each wave, I have seen tremendous transformation and miracles, both in myself and in the Church. And with every revival, creative miracles abound in greater measure.

Revival brings floods of God's mercy and grace. It also brings the quality of His presence, goodness and power to another level. We are to take God's power outside the four walls of the church—into the marketplace, into our cities and into all the nations of the earth. We need to thank God for each outpouring of His Spirit.

Do Everything for the Glory of God

Finally, whatever you do, do it all for the glory of God (see 1 Corinthians 10:31). We are to do everything for His glory. Indeed, we are to live to bring glory to His name through our bodies, souls and spirits.

For some of us, glorifying God with our body may mean eating better and exercising more often. For others, glorifying God with our soul may mean seeking inner healing or deliverance for addictions or other types of persistent problems. For those who have not received salvation, God receives glory when they accept His gift of salvation and give Him their lives and hearts.

Do you know whose image you are made in? The Bible says we were made in the image of God (see Genesis 1:26). Because of this, we must render our hearts and lives to God and dedicate ourselves to bringing Him glory. We were bought with a price, so our lives are not our own (see 1 Corinthians 6:19–20). Therefore, we need to faithfully and wisely steward the life He gave us.

This principle is illustrated in Matthew 22, when the Pharisees tried to trick Jesus by asking Him, "Is it right to pay taxes to Caesar or not?" Jesus understood that they had framed the question to put him in a no-win position. If He answered "yes," the Pharisees could tell the Jews that Jesus was in alliance with the Romans. If He answered "no," the Pharisees could tell the Romans that Jesus was in rebellion against Rome's authority. Either way, they could accuse Jesus and turn people against Him.

Jesus turned their attempt to trap Him into an opportunity to demonstrate that being created in God's image means we are God's and owe Him our entire lives. Being infinitely wise, Jesus asked the Pharisees to show Him the coin used for paying the tax. Then He asked them, "Whose portrait is this? And whose inscription?" (Matthew 22:19-20).

The Pharisees responded, "Caesar's."

Jesus said to them, "Give to Caesar what is Caesar's, and to God what is God's" (Matthew 22:21). The simple principle He stated had profound implications. Jesus knew the Pharisees were consumed with appearances and maintaining their positions and prestige. They gave lip service to God, but their hearts were elsewhere. They were not giving to God what is God's. They were going through the motions of dedicated service and stewardship to God in their duties in the Temple, but His glory and praise were not the central purpose of their lives. In one sentence, Jesus not only deftly handled their tax question, but He also challenged the Pharisees by revealing to them the condition of their hearts!

God calls us to dedicate our entire lives to His glory, for He knows when we glorify Him, we find our highest fulfillment and joy. Yet the Lord not only calls us to praise Him, He also glorifies and blesses us when we do. And He shares His glory with us so we can enjoy it and reflect it back to Him (see John 17:22). When we glorify God, we simply become more glorious. And the more glorious we become, the more we can glorify God with our entire being. David sings, "Glorify the LORD with me; let us exalt his name together. . . . Those who look to him are radiant; their faces are never covered with shame" (Psalm 34:3, 5).

As we worship God and glorify His name, His glory comes upon us and transforms us into the image of Christ. This process continues until the final day, when all heaven and earth will be filled with the glory of God. Until that day, I pray that you will receive the fullness of the glory of God, becoming the light of the world as you reflect His glory into the darkness, and ultimately bring Him glory through all you do.

Notes

Chapter 1 What Is Glory?

1. Kris Vallotton, *Developing a Supernatural Lifestyle: A Practical Guide to a Life of Signs, Wonders and Miracles* (Shippensburg, Pa.: Destiny Image, 2007), 205.

Chapter 2 Glory as the Manifest Presence of God

1. John Arnott, *The Father's Blessing* (Lake Mary, Fla.: Charisma House, 1995). John Arnott, *Experience the Blessing: Testimonies from Toronto* (Ventura, Calif.: Renew Books, 2001).

Chapter 3 Glory as the Revealed Goodness of God

1. Robert Lewis and Wayne Cordeiro, *The Culture Shift* (New York: Jossey-Bass, 2005), 1–2.

Chapter 4 Glory as the Resurrection Power of God

1. This and a number of other healing miracles, resurrections and creative signs and wonders are thoroughly researched and documented by Jane Rumph in her book, *Signs and Wonders in America Today: Amazing Accounts of God's Power* (Ann Arbor, Mich.: Servant Publications, 2003).

Chapter 8 How to Receive More Glory

1. Fred and Sharon Wright, *The World's Greatest Revivals* (Shippensburg, Pa.: Destiny Image, 2007), 161–62.

Chapter 10 The Glory of God and Apostolic Alignment

1. Arthur Wallis, *In the Day of Thy Power* (Christian Literature Crusade, 1956), 10.

2. Peter Wagner, *Dominion* (Grand Rapids: Chosen Books, 2008).

3. Kris Vallotton and Bill Johnson, *The Supernatural Ways of Royalty* (Shippensburg, Pa.: Destiny Image, 2006), 137–38.

4. Ibid.

Chapter 11 The Glory of God and Transformation

1. Meaghan S. McCormick, "The Great Awakening and Its Effects on the Society and Religion of the Connecticut River Valley," http://www.long meadow.org/hist_soc/awakening.htm.

2. Barbara Cross, "William Wilberforce 1759–1833," www.britannica .com/bios/wilberforce.html.

3. Ken Curtis, Ph.D., Joe Thomas, Ph.D., Tracey L. Craig, and Ann T. Snyder, "The Fight Against Slavery and What We Can Learn From It," Chris tian History Institute, http://www.christianhistorytimeline.com/GLIMPSEF/ Glimpses2/glimpses200.html.

4. "The Second Great Awakening," Christian History Institute, http://www .christianhistorytimeline.com/GLIMPSEF/Glimpses/glmps040.shtml.

5. "The Haystack Revival: A Devotional Guide, Introduction and Back-ground," http://www.students.org/prayer/Haystack%20Awakening%202006 .pdf.

6. Barry Manuel, "The Pensacola Outpouring: The Father's Blessing for the '90s," John Mark Ministries, http://www.jmm.aaa.net.au/articles/8955 .htm.

7. J. Gilchrist Lawson, "Charles Finney: A Brief Biography," from *Deeper Experiences of Famous Christians*, http://www.CharlesGFinney.com/law sonbio.htm.

8. S. J. Hill, "Hearts on Fire," from *Personal Revival*, http://www.fathers glory.com/media/Personal_Revival-Chapter_One-Hill.pdf.

9. James Autry, "Understanding the Seven Mountains," http://www .restoreamerica.org/pdf/Understanding%20the%20Seven%20Mountains. pdf.

Chapter 12 The Glory of God and the Transfer of Wealth

1. "Host Bio: Pat Robertson," The 700 Club, http://www.cbn.com/700club/ showinfo/staff/patrobertson.aspx

2. "Salvation Army Receives $1.5 Billion Bequest," MSNBC, http://www .msnbc.msn.com/id/4006823/.

3. Suzanne Woodley, Bremen Leak, and Danna Cook, "The Top Givers," *BusinessWeek*, November 27, 2006.

4. "Interview with Abraham Alex Tanuseputra," *United World*, December 20, 2004.

5. "Transformed by Christ: A Brief History of the Worldwide Church of God," *Worldwide Church of God*, July 7, 2008.

About the Author

Ché Ahn (M.Div. and D.Min., Fuller Theological Seminary) is the senior pastor of Harvest Rock Church in Pasadena, California, a vibrant multiethnic congregation dedicated to fulfilling the Great Commandment and the Great Commission. He is also the president and founder of Harvest International Ministry, an apostolic network of more than 5,500 churches in more than 35 nations. He served as president of The Call from 1999–2003. The author of numerous books, Ché travels and teaches extensively throughout the world. He and his wife, Sue, have four adult children who love Jesus. For more information about his ministry, go to www.CheAhn.org.